The L
JOHN YOUNG

The Life and Times of
JOHN YOUNG

Confidant and Advisor
to Kamehameha the Great

Emmett Cahill

ISLAND HERITAGE
PUBLISHING

©1999 Island Heritage Publishing
All rights reserved. Except for brief passages quoted in a review, no part of this book may be reproduced in any form or by any means, electronic or mechanical, including photocopying and recording, or by an information storage and retrieval system, without permission in writing from the publisher.

Written by Emmett Cahill
Illustrated by Herb Kawainui Kāne
Edited by Virginia Wageman
Book and cover design by Jim Wageman, Wigwag

ISLAND HERITAGE
PUBLISHING

99-880 Iwaena Street
Aiea, Hawai'i 96701
808 · 487 · 7299

Printed in Hong Kong
ISBN 0-89610-449-4

Contents

Illustrations

 *Preface*

It was said by sea captains of the time, and historians of the present agree, that the names of Kamehameha the Great and John Young come up more frequently than any others during the period from 1790 to 1835. Enough information exists about Kamehameha to fill volumes in local libraries. Conversely, there is so little written about John Young, except in a few brief articles in early periodicals, that would-be biographers have passed him by. One well-known author of Hawaiiana decided against doing a story on Young because, according to this person, there is so little to write about him.

When I have replied to inquiries about what I was writing, the reaction frequently has been, "Oh, John Young, the Honolulu artist! That should be interesting." That venerable gentleman died recently in his eighties and his biography will indeed be interesting. The point is that few have ever heard of the John Young of early Hawai'i, despite the fact that he was an advisor to the first sovereign of the Hawaiian Islands.

The search for information on Young's life has been long and laborious. It all goes back as much as a couple hundred years ago. What records were kept then were often by sea captains, some more informative than others, but few so enlightening as those of Captain George Vancouver. It seems that all sea captains who found their way to Hawai'i ended up writing a history of their journeys with a generic title such as "The History of a Voyage around the World." Young drew brief attention from some of them. Regrettably, such other records of the time, some by Young himself and a few by other contemporaries, were lost to history by acts of God, such as floods or termites, or just by poor safekeeping. What exists is in bits and pieces, and bit by bit, piece by piece, a picture of a good man has come into focus.

The search meant looking under many rocks to see what lay beneath. It was always rewarding to find a second rock under the first, for it often revealed hidden gems. Also, helpful friends and Hawaiiana colleagues came forth with hitherto unknown or unappreciated tidbits. Gradually a picture was framed of an English sailor who in midlife, either directly or indirectly, was involved in major happenings that became bookends for the final days of dictatorship and the establishment of the Hawaiian monarchy.

It is relatively clear now just what the man did, for that is drawn from such records as exist. What sort of man he was has to be somewhat conjectured. It has been said that he was taciturn and that he wisely never interfered with the affairs of the chiefs under Kamehameha. The decisions he made on behalf of his king were sagacious. He was a good listener say some of the visitors who chronicled their brief stays. The record shows that he was an exemplary family man. True to his wife and concerned with the upbringing of his six children, he was temperate in his tastes. Unlike the pattern of so many white men who settled in southern isles, he did not, as the saying goes, exploit the natives. His conduct and service merited his being honored as a high chief. He was, after forty-five years of service, interred at the age of ninety-one among other high chiefs and sovereigns in Hawai'i's Royal Mausoleum.

What is set forth is not a social study of Polynesian culture or changing times. It is simply the story of a good and fair individual who was an unwitting agent for change in Hawai'i's history. We can regret that some of Young's life still lies buried in the mists and whispers of the past.

⚜ Acknowledgments

I am unsure whether I owe Scott Stone any thanks for persuading me to write the story of the hitherto unpublished life of John Young. Nonetheless, Scott, the author of seven novels and ten nonfiction books, and the former city editor of the *Honolulu Advertiser,* patiently read and critiqued each chapter as it was turned out and then the complete manuscript before submission to the publisher. I am grateful for his guidance, expertise, and friendship.

The story of John Young would only be half-told, and then not in proper style, had it not been for the input and genuine interest I received from Dorothy Barrere. Not only is she an anthropologist retired after forty years with Bishop Museum, she is also one of eleven individuals recognized by the Hawaiian Historical Society in its centennial year (1992) as a Distinguished Living Historian. Dorothy possesses an abundance of knowledge about Hawaiian history of John Young's time, and she shared it with me generously, filling in gaps, suggesting subjects, correcting spelling, and checking dates. She also contributed much to the length and accuracy of the bibliography and shared with me related books from her Hawaiiana library. Also, I should not overlook her ability to read and write Hawaiian.

It is through the superb period illustrations by artist, author, and Polynesia historian Herb Kawainui Kāne that John Young comes to life in this book. I am grateful not only for his artistry but also for his providing answers to many questions and turning over to me a number of copies of ship captains' logs and related historical gems.

Months of search were eased by help from the Hawaiian Mission Children's Society through its librarian, Marilyn Reppun. Similarly, I owe much to Barbara Dunn, director of the Hawaiian Historical Society, who was always patient and gracious in responding to my many reference requests. At Bishop Museum the personal help from archivists Neena Sachdeva and Stuart Ching was considerable. The treasures of the Hawai'i State Archives were made easier to find thanks to Geoffrey White, Victoria Nihi, Mary Ann Akao, and former staff member Richard Thompson. I was also fortunate in having access to the books in the University of Hawai'i–Hilo (Mookini) Library. The reference department of the Hilo Public Library was also most helpful in my John Young search.

I am grateful to Paul Dahlquist, director of Lyman Memorial Museum, for critiquing my first draft. His background as an anthropologist in the area of Hawaiian history and culture provided authenticity. I owe special thanks to my friend Mary Rentz, who, on her days off from the Hawaiʻi Public Library System, was a willing and capable researcher in each of the above-mentioned libraries. Terry KuʻAuhau Wallace, author and historian, contributed much of the information on Young's colleague Isaac Davis.

Early in the project I received a bonanza from George Collins, Jr., of Kailua-Kona. He turned over to me a sizable box of his father's many notes and drafts, all relative to Young's history. Collins Sr. had planned to write a book on the subject, but he died before it could be accomplished.

Laura Carter Schuster, on the staff of the Hawaiʻi National Park, was a source of valuable information on the Young homestead at Kawaihae. Also accommodating were National Park Service personnel Daniel Kawaiaea and Ernest Young of the Puʻukoholā park. Likewise I am in debt to the Daughters of Hawaiʻi who generously provided items of genuine interest concerning the life of Queen Emma, granddaughter of John Young.

I am especially grateful to the board of directors of the Lyman Memorial Museum for their financial support. Generous support also came from the Queen Emma Foundation as well as the McInerny Trust and the Robert E. Black Foundation. I extend special *mahalo* to friend Susan Johnson who encouraged me early on to seek grants.

Others whose input and interest helped make this work possible include Gavan Daws (also recognized as a Distinguished Living Historian) and Dr. Jack Lockwood, volcanologist of renown. Information concerning diacritics was provided by Kiapo Perreira, Hawaiian Studies faculty member at University of Hawaiʻi–Hilo.

To those whom I have inadvertently overlooked (and whose names will flash before me as soon as this book is off the press) my sincere thanks and apologies.

Prologue

It was an often-repeated picture: a visiting vessel with tall sails standing just offshore of a small Hawaiian seacoast community. Between it and the shore were dozens of canoes filled with natives eager to trade fruit and vegetables for such articles as nails, cloth, tools, iron, and other artifacts. On board the ship were white sailors and officers equally willing to replenish their supply of fruit, vegetables, pork, fresh water, and wood for fuel.

Frequently the chief of the village would be among the Hawaiians who saw this as a festive occasion. It was on such a day in early March of 1790 that a high chief named Kameʻeiamoku ventured out to a brig named the *Eleanora,* which lay off the small village of Kaʻūpūlehu on the northwest coast of Hawaiʻi Island, the largest and most southerly of the Hawaiian archipelago. This ship, of a type sometimes known as a "snow," would be long remembered, but for all the wrong reasons.[1]

Accompanied by his retinue, Kameʻeiamoku made his way with other curious and hospitable Hawaiians to the *Eleanora,* likely to engage in trading. Having boarded the vessel, Kameʻeiamoku apparently did something that obviously annoyed the *Eleanora*'s skipper, Simon Metcalfe, a man easy to irritate and a bad one to cross. He was never known to be friendly with the islanders, and in fact he had a reputation for insisting that he and his authority be recognized.

As a chief himself, Kameʻeiamoku considered himself the captain's equal. Hawaiian chiefs were not known for their reserve, so perhaps it was something the chief said or did that provoked Metcalfe. It might have been that the chief violated a minor ship's rule, or he may have touched something that made him suspect of thievery. Whatever that detail may be, it is recorded by historian W. D. Alexander, and other historians, that the high chief "was insulted and beaten with a rope's end by Metcalfe for some trifling offense."[2]

Simon Metcalfe would have had no way of seeing the future, but those blows, which so embarrassed a chief in front of his people, would be repaid, with interest, by Kameʻeiamoku. The beating triggered reactions that indirectly altered Hawaiʻi's history and directly impacted the lives of the British sailor John Young and his contemporaries.

❦ Chronology

1744   March 17: John Young born in Great Crosby, Lancashire, England.

1787   February: Young signs aboard the vessel *Eleanora* in New York City, with Simon Metcalfe as his captain.[1]

June: The *Eleanora* lays over in Batavia (Jakarta) until early August.

August: The *Eleanora* arrives at Macao and Canton.

1788   March: The *Eleanora* sails for the American Northwest to trade.

August: The *Eleanora* returns to China, having replenished in the Sandwich Islands.

December 9: Pirates storm the *Eleanora* outside Macao at Lark's Bay, killing two crewmen and causing extensive damage.

1789   January: The *Eleanora* sails for Kamchatka for fur and sealskins.

March: The *Eleanora* returns from Siberia. Metcalfe purchases the *Fair American,* naming his son Thomas captain and Isaac Davis first mate.

June 5: The *Eleanora* and the *Fair American* sail for the American Northwest for trading, becoming separated early on due to a storm off Japan.

Early November: The *Eleanora* sets sail for the Sandwich Islands to rendezvous with the *Fair American* and replenish before returning to China.

1790   January: The *Eleanora* sails from Kealakekua, on Hawai'i Island's western coast, for Maui to get fresh water while waiting for the *Fair American.*

January/February: Theft of a cutter leads to the Olowalu Massacre.

Mid-March: The *Fair American* is attacked off north Hawai'i Island. All are killed except Davis, who is taken ashore and cared for.

March 17: Young goes ashore on Hawai'i Island to hunt birds; natives prevent him from returning to his ship for fear that he will tell Metcalfe of the attack on the *Fair American.* (Young had no knowledge of the attack.)

March 18 or 19: Young meets Kamehameha, who promises to care for and protect him. They then meet Davis, who is recovering from his wounds.

Spring: Battle of the Red-Mouth Gun off Waimanu, where Young and Davis carry out an attack from the *Fair American*. In the Maui Battle of Iao Valley, Young and Davis help bring victory with the cannon Lopaka from the *Fair American*. They are also engaged in East Hawai'i skirmishes with an enemy chief, Keōua.

November: From Kawaihae, Young sights the eruption of Kiluaea Volcano.

1790–91	Kamehameha constructs Pu'ukoholā, one of the largest temples in Polynesia.
1791	April: Attempted escape by Young and Davis is thwarted.
1793	February: Young has the first of two visits with Captain George Vancouver. Young makes his home in Kawaihae, one of several large tracts of land bestowed upon him by Kamehameha. His is thought to be the first stone house in the Islands.
1795	Battle of O'ahu in Nu'uanu Valley, where Young and Davis help bring victory with European arms and strategies. Young marries Namokuelua, a young O'ahu woman.
1802–12	Young is governor of Hawai'i Island.
1804	Namokuelua dies, having given birth to two boys, Robert and James Kānehoa.
1806	Young marries a niece of Kamehameha named Kaoanaeha, who gives birth to one son and three daughters: Fanny (Pane) Kakelaokalani, Grace Kama'iku'i, Keoni Ana (John Jr.), and Jane (Gini or Kini) Lahilahi. Kaoanaeha dies in 1850.
1810	April: Isaac Davis dies, presumably poisoned by affronted chiefs.
1812	Young is governor of O'ahu for a year or less.
1819	May: Kamehameha the Great dies, with Young, his "favorite foreigner," at his side. August: A portrait of Young is sketched by an artist from the French vessel *Uranie*.
1833	Young goes to live in Honolulu with his daughter Grace and son-in-law Dr. Thomas C. B. Rooke.
1835	December 16: Young dies at Rooke's home at age ninety-one. He is buried on December 18 at Pohukaina, Hawai'i's mausoleum for royalty and chiefs.
1866	October: Young's body is transferred to the new Royal Mausoleum, Mauna Ala, in Nu'uanu Valley.

The Life and Times of
JOHN YOUNG

Molokai

Maui

Kahoolawe

Hawaii

Waipi'o Valley

Kawaihae

Ka'ūpūlehu   Waimea

MAUNA
KEA

Kailua   Hilo

Kona
DISTRICT

Kealakekua

MAUNA
LOA

1 ❖ The World of 1744

Events in Europe in the middle of the eighteenth century reflected internal strife and social change, as sovereigns sought to expand their power and individuals broke with convention. In small towns men stood on the edges, looked beyond, and wondered.

John Wesley rode through England on horseback to organize Methodist societies and to hold the first conference of this new religious sect.

A Scotsman named Serson pioneered the gyroscope, an instrument that would, years later, advance the course of navigation. It was a significant matter for the great seaport of Liverpool.

Sotheby's, the renowned art auction house, had its beginnings in London when the library of a local physician sold for 826 pounds.

A pogrom to drive the Jews out of Bohemia and Moravia was launched by Queen Maria Theresa of Austria.

Piracy on the high seas peaked in 1744, when ruthless corsairs plundered the ships of any nation.

In the Americas, the colonists were becoming restless and chaffing as the British bit tightened. In Virginia, a year earlier, a baby named Thomas was born to the Jeffersons.

In England the birth of the Industrial Revolution saw a transition from rural areas to newly sprung-up factory towns, where men from field and farm found new work amid smelters and smoke.

Half an unknown world away, a much more serene and uninterrupted way of life was enjoyed by several thousand Polynesians who lived in a chain of verdant and breeze-blessed islands in the middle of the world's mightiest ocean, the misnamed Pacific. It would be thirty-four years before their lifestyle was altered forever through the chance discovery of Hawai'i by Great Britain's Captain James Cook.

It was March 17 of 1744 in the town of Great Crosby, in England's Lancashire County, that a son was born to Robert and Grace Young. They named him John.

Great Crosby was actually a small village, and adjacent to it was Little Crosby. Both were located about a mile in from the Irish Sea and half a dozen miles from Liverpool (today both communities are part of Greater Liverpool). The community held little for its male inhabitants other than farming, a precarious occupation. The young males of the area were often drawn to the seaport city of Liverpool, where farm boys became seafarers or shipbuilders, even masters in the maritime trade. The city, located on the wide estuary of the Mersey River, provided easy access to the Irish Sea and from there to the rest of the globe. The port, with its adjacent shipbuilding facilities, was already a maritime center of great repute, hustle, and bustle. Its miles of docks saw cargo-laden ships come from and go to all major ports of the world. The great seaport lent its name to what was called the "Liverpool House," which Webster's dictionary describes as "a midship superstructure extending from side to side to provide a bridge deck."

Among the Lancashire lads who looked to Liverpool for a livelihood were Peter and James, two older sons of Robert and Grace Young. Both young men became Liverpool pilots.[1]

Records of John's life prior to 1790 are murky. Despite thorough searches of maritime records in Liverpool,[2] the records of Sefton parish, and civil records of Crosby, nothing has been found to throw any light on the life of Robert Young and his family.

Judging from portions of journals John kept later in life, his education was limited, perhaps the equivalent of sixth grade in the Crosby schoolhouse. From his later use of the Bible and the copying of a Christian poem, it is evident that he had not only the ability to write but also a connection with the current religion of the area, which most likely was Anglican or Methodist.

It is speculated that he, like his two older brothers, found his way to Liverpool and the life of a seafarer. The speculation sees him beginning as a cabin boy, perhaps at twelve years of age. He could well have advanced to an apprentice seaman in the Seven Years' War against France, and to a full-fledged privateersman in the war with the American colonies. The question is which side he fought for. Nonetheless, he was a country boy who became a skilled boatswain, which led him to become an advisor to a great Hawaiian king.

2 ❁ Enter the Eleanora

Details of the first half of John Young's long ninety-one-year life are not only vague and obscure, they are absent except for his birth. Nothing else emerges with a certainty until March of 1790, when at the age of forty-six he was stranded on Hawai'i Island. During his last years he apparently recorded on paper enough about his life to fill a book. In his failing years, in 1833, Young went to live with his daughter Grace and her husband, Dr. Thomas C. B. Rooke, a prominent physician in Honolulu. The doctor's residence was in the central part of the city. It is known that Rooke had some of Young's papers, which he later turned over to the Archives of Hawai'i, but at some point a flood washed away Young's precious memoirs. This probably occurred at the end of the nineteenth century, when Young had been dead more than sixty years and Rooke for about thirty years.[1] It is uncertain precisely where in Honolulu the flood occurred or who was custodian of the Young papers at the time.

The only major hint of Young's early life is found in an article titled "John Young, As Told to Captain Charles H. Barnard in 1816 by John Young Himself."[2] Young was seventy-two years old when he spun that story. In recounting his life for Barnard, Young begins (or Barnard begins it for him) by telling of the time when he was probably in his early or mid-forties and he joined the ship *Eleanora*, the vessel which ultimately landed him in Hawai'i forever.

Told in the first person, it commences with Young saying: "Twenty-five years ago I entered as Boatswain on board an American ship, Captain Medcalf [*sic*] who was bound on a trading voyage to the North-West Coast. On our passage, we touched at this island [Hawai'i] for refreshments." The only other clue he gives about the ship's course is that they had carried a cargo of furs to Canton.

When Young said that it was twenty-five years ago that he joined Metcalfe's ship (the *Eleanora*) he was perhaps rounding out the years, or perhaps Barnard did it in the retelling. Twenty-five years prior to 1816 would have been 1791, by which time Young had been in Hawai'i a full year and the *Eleanora* had long since gone back to China and then to the sub-Antarctic Ocean.

The *New York Daily Advertiser* of February 18, 1787, reported that on the previous day Metcalfe had obtained clearance at the New York Customs House "for the brig *Eleanora* . . . [to set sail] for Madeira and the East Indies."

Prior to Young's service on the brig, where he would hold the important post of boatswain, we can only speculate. In August 1856 the United States commissioner to Hawai'i, David L. Gregg, responded to an inquiry from a Colonel W. P. Young, of Washington, D.C., on the subject of John Young's ancestry and lineage. Gregg wrote: "For these particulars I am chiefly indebted to Dr. T. C. B. Rooke, who is married to a daughter of John Young and possesses most of the papers left to him." Gregg's letter states that "prior to our revolution he [Young] went to the North American Colonies and was engaged as a seaman chiefly from the Ports of New York & Philadelphia."[3] However, it is quite clear from information about the last part of Young's life, while he was in Hawai'i, that he was considered an Englishman in every sense. He may have remained a Loyalist, but in 1787, four years after the war's end, he was able to sign on an American ship.

A big question mark rises here. Where was the *Eleanora* when Young signed on? Was she in New York, departing in 1787? Or was Young in Macao in June 1789, when the *Eleanora* sailed from there for the American Northwest? We know from Metcalfe's letter of March 22, 1790, that Young was his boatswain when he was stranded on Hawai'i Island.[4] Unfortunately, the log of the *Eleanora* was lost with the ship when it went down in 1793 off the island of Kerguelen in the southern Indian Ocean.

The few followers of John Young's life are divided on the matter. Those who believe that Young sailed out of New York base their premise on Gregg's statement that Young "was engaged as a seaman chiefly from the Ports of New York & Philadelphia. In the winter of 1789–90 he left the United States on the ship *Eleanor*."[5] The problem is that this date is two years later than that published in the 1787 *New York Daily Advertiser.*[6]

Those who believe that Young sailed on the *Eleanora* out of Macao in 1789 rely on information from the journal of Captain James Colnett that gives credence to their belief. In his journal, Colnett writes that he lost his boatswain to the *Eleanora* in Macao in 1789, and many believe that this boatswain was John Young.[7]

As for the 190-ton brig *Eleanora,* details are lacking regarding her origins, but she can be said to have led an adventurous life. Naval archives identify her as having been a British troop transport captained by Arthur Rayburn in 1776.[8] She was acquired after the war by a consortium of New

York businessmen at the urging of Simon Metcalfe, a one-time Yankee landowner of considerable means who was an entrepreneur and an American revolutionist. She was converted to a merchant ship, and sometime after 1785 Metcalfe persuaded the New York owners to let him captain the ship and enter the growing fur trade in the American Northwest.[9] The vessel must have had another name prior to its change of owners, for Metcalfe had it named *Eleanora*, after his wife. The New York investors staked Metcalfe and expected to share in the sale of a cargo of thirteen thousand sealskins that another merchant had acquired in the Falkland Islands. Metcalfe bought them for fifty cents a skin, knowing that a lucrative market awaited him in far-off Cathay.[10]

Regardless of whether John Young joined the *Eleanora* out of New York or Macao, it was Metcalfe's good fortune to find a sailor the likes of Young, who qualified as a boatswain. Webster's dictionary gives a rather prosaic description of the role of this important individual: "A warrant officer on a warship, or a petty officer on a merchant ship in charge of rigging, anchors, cable etc." It was, and is, a key position, and one with considerable responsibilities, perhaps more so in the eighteenth century than today.

The boatswains of John Young's day had one thing in common: they were an uncommon lot, and a most valuable one. The vast experiences of the British maritime services had, by the fading days of the eighteenth century, shaped the duties of each member of a ship's company to the point where every man signing on board a vessel knew his duties and what to expect. One man knew it all: the boatswain, frequently shortened to bosun (which is how boatswain is pronounced). He was neither officer nor crew, but something in between. He could be a companion or a confidant to either the ship's commander or its crew, without abusing the privilege. He could be the conduit for the captain's orders to the crew, and he could be the man who, often with taste and subtlety, brought the crew's complaints to the attention of one of the officers. He was the equivalent of today's warrant officer, and while he was something less than a commissioned officer, he was much more than a man who sailed before the mast. What made the boatswain a standout on any vessel was that he probably knew more about things involving the ship as a whole than anyone aboard.

Normally the boatswain's duties involved the deck division—the people involved with actually running the ship, keeping it shipshape, keeping the deck itself, the ship's boats, the rigging, etc., all in proper working order. But since a ship was sort of an ecosystem in and of itself, nothing taking place in one part of the vessel went unnoticed by all others, nor did any happening fail to impact on the ship as a whole. The boatswain, then, kept an eye on *all* of it. For example, if the vessel were a warship, or carried any kind of defensive cannon, the ship would have a gunner and sailors assigned to man the guns in combat. But because the working of the guns impacted on the conditions of the deck, the disturbance of other duties, the storage of powder and shot, the boatswain would be concerned, hence much involved. If he were typical the boatswain would know the gunner's problems and in time would know the gunner's job.

A good boatswain was a most valuable asset aboard a ship and might be called upon to supervise many things not otherwise precisely defined. He might advise the captain that the sail maker's canvas was not up to standards; he might tell the captain or first mate that the crew's food was insufficient to curb scurvy before the voyage was over. He might advise the young cabin-boy as to which crewmen to avoid and which would play good-natured pranks. He might decide when the crew's bedding was in need of airing, or advise the ship's officers on the status of water rations.

The boatswain was, in effect, the man who made things happen aboard the ship. The captain issued orders and assumed they would be obeyed. The first mate was usually a substitute for the captain, on watch when the captain rested. The second mate was generally a jack-of-all trades, like the boatswain, with the additional knowledge of navigation, which made him an officer. All officers, if they followed tradition, dealt with the boatswain where possible, instead of going to the crew. The boatswain himself could have an assistant or two, depending on the size of the ship. A very large one would have boatswain's mates who stood deck watches, and, with the thin, shrill boatswain's pipe, would send the crew to their duties or to their meals, etc., with the recognizable whistling of the pipe. Like their boatswain, they would be expected to keep an eye on the ship as a whole, to note discrepancies or irregularities among the crew or deficiencies of the ship itself.

No doubt some boatswains were ambitious; all of them began as ordinary seamen and climbed to their positions of authority. And some of them aspired to be a ship's officer and became so. Some large ships could have a master-at-arms, which was, in effect, the chief of police aboard the vessel. With this personage maintaining discipline, the boatswain could concentrate on the important tasks of keeping the ship in good condition and the crew responding properly. Without a master-at-arms, discipline often fell to the boatswain, who added it to his already long chore list. A wise boatswain tried to see that discipline infractions by the crew never reached the eyes or ears of the officers, who would be more severe in their punishment. Thus a boatswain was often hated by the crew for enforcing rules. He was also respected by crewmen for keeping them from a flogging or other severe punishment.

John Young was a good boatswain—an outstanding sailor, a dedicated part of the ship's company, and a man of action and intelligence. The boatswain stood with his feet in two worlds, the officers' and the crew's. But his job was to keep the vessel shipshape and seaworthy. It could be a daunting task, but a lot of good men were equal to it.

3 ❖ Tracking the Trader

As anxious as Metcalfe was to get into trading, and hopefully recoup some of the great losses he had suffered during the revolution, his investors were equally anxious for him to get underway and return with handsome profits. A competent crew was gathered, the ship was provisioned, and on February 17 the New York Customs House issued a clearance. With the captain were his sons Robert and Thomas, both in their late teens. The *Eleanora* sailed out of New York Harbor on February 18, 1787, plagued by the typically raw and cold north Atlantic winter weather. But in another week the skies softened as the ship dipped down ten degrees latitude, then headed due east for its first stop, Madeira. The ship would not be in cold waters again for another year. Madeira, a refreshment station with a pleasing climate, gave the crew a few days of rest as its famed red wine and other provisions were loaded. In all likelihood Young, having already been a seaman for perhaps as many as twenty-seven years, had visited the Portuguese Madeira Islands, but under whose flag remains a question.

In a matter of a week or less the *Eleanora* sailed deeper into southern waters, soon rounding Africa's Cape of Good Hope. That was an area that Metcalfe decided to avoid out of mistrust of the Dutch, and being a frugal man, he feared their high port fees. Now it was time to head into the Indian Ocean, first by sailing up Africa's east coast. There, between Mozambique and the island of Madagascar, they found the refreshment station of Mohili in the small Comoro Islands.[1]

A couple of weeks later Metcalfe began his long trip up the east coast of the subcontinent of India. (There were likely other stops on India's west side, but they are unknown, owing to the loss of the log.) He stopped at Karikal, a small port, one of scores along that crowded coast. A day or so after Karikal, the *Eleanora* sailed into the frequented port of Pondicherry. Then it went on to Madras, one of the biggest cities in southeast India. It was at Madras that two of Metcalfe's officers left him, reportedly unhappy with his penchant for punishment and cruelty. Madras was the *Eleanora*'s last recorded stop before entering the wide Hooghly River at the mouth of the mighty Ganges for the sixty-mile trip to Calcutta. This teeming city of one hundred thousand people was sultry, dirty, and crowded, except for where the British Fort William and its soldiers' barracks were located. Elsewhere Young and his mates would, in their free time, see little but crowds of native Indians in a sea of shanties and mediocre shops. Metcalfe spent at least a month in the city, hobnobbing with European officers, traders, speculators, and merchants. It was an opportune time to have copper sheathing affixed to the vessel, which was being attacked by the destructive teredos, or wood-worms. It was also at Calcutta that Metcalfe was informed that his was the first American ship to enter the city.[2]

Leaving this northern India metropolis on the Bay of Bengal, the *Eleanora* was pointed south again. It would make two or more stops before it reached the island of Ceylon, where it anchored in Trinkmale Bay on the island's northeast coast. The Dutch, who then controlled the island, were skeptical that such a small vessel could have made it there all the way from New York. Then it was down to the East Indies, a trip that began at the upper end of the long Strait of Malacca. The *Eleanora* sailed in the company of at least one other vessel, which served as protection from the corsairs that roamed the waters. Batavia (present day Jakarta) was Metcalfe's midsummer goal, and it was also the apex of the spice islands route sailed principally by Portuguese and Dutch traders. The city, which the *Eleanora* reached in late June, was hot, like other ports they had touched, and it was also a steamy, malarial city. By that time they had been five months at sea. (Had they arrived two years later they would have met Captain Bligh of *Bounty* fame.)

One month after weighing anchor at Batavia, on August 8, 1787, the *Eleanora* sailed into the small Portuguese community of Macao, at the mouth of the Pearl River estuary leading to Canton.[3] This last leg of the month-long trip had taken them through many islands in the South China Sea. The ship had been gone six months and had traveled more than ten thousand miles in the Atlantic, the Indian, and the Pacific oceans. Macao was an essential stop for traders, for it was there that permits were given to travel up the Pearl to Canton.

The Portuguese had held Macao for 230 years, since 1557, but Chinese officialdom controlled the part of the small peninsula near the mouth of the Pearl River. The eighty-mile trip on the river to Canton was a welcome respite for Young and his fellow seamen. Traveling was slow because the river was afloat with vessels of every size and shape. There were barges loaded with cargo coming and going, and sampans on which whole families lived, often with animals. There were great junks, their full sails carrying families of the wealthy, dignitaries, and supplies. Fishermen abounded. Both sides of the river bore the riches of alluvial soil washed down from inland provinces. Rice paddies, gardens of vegetables, and fruit orchards were in abundance. It was a populous area along the riverbanks, speckled with small villages consisting of houses made of stone, brick, and mud.

Just short of Canton was the busy port of Whampoa, where most traders anchored and proceeded to meet their agents in Canton. On the approach to the city were compounds called factories: the warehouses, the offices, and often the palatial residences of the trading companies. Canton itself, with a teeming population of half a million people, was China's only open city, where foreign ships came to trade for tea, silks, and porcelain. A large wall enclosing the metropolis saw to it that trading was done at the factors, near the river. The outer city was the only part of China that was not off limits to "foreign devils." John Young and his companions who enjoyed shore leave found the Chinese as different as they had found the Bengalis from the Indonesians. Here they were treated to the jostling traffic of the rickshas, the temples that rose above the skyline, the wailing and singing and the clanging of cymbals that marked a Chinese funeral procession down a crowded thoroughfare—it was all part of the pulse of a thriving Oriental city. There were the grog shops and fleshpots that offered a sailor release from his stress—and his hard-earned wages.

The thirteen thousand furs that Metcalfe had gambled on for only fifty cents each brought him a windfall. Furs were becoming popular among the wealthy Chinese, and he received the munificent sum of $65,000! Five dollars a pelt. He would never again be so fortunate.

Once the business of unloading the cargo of furs was complete, there would be the tediously slow trip down the Pearl to Macao. More business would be conducted at that station with as many as three dozen vessels at anchor. Now was the time for refitting those vessels, which had ended voyages of thousands of miles, by loading such cargo as tea and silks for the ready European buyers and a fast-growing American market. Macao layovers were often long, an opportunity for Simon Metcalfe and his two sons to mix with officers of other ships, and possibly with some of the well-to-do Portuguese who lived along the tree-lined promenades. The small city had a European air about it, with its white-painted homes and a 160-year-old Catholic cathedral. The city's citadel looked over all of it. It was a good "walk-around" community for sailors who had found no such luxury in the walled city of Canton.

Metcalfe, now with ample funds, had the *Eleanora* thoroughly refitted prior to the long trip to the American Northwest in early 1788. It would be his first visit to that upper west corner of the continent of North America, and he had learned that there was indeed a rich market in China for the skins of sea otter and seals. Quoting historian Judge F. W. Howay, Rhys Richards writes: "Metcalfe certainly had the time, the money and access to the necessary sources of information to make a brief trip to the Northwest coast during 1788."[4] Metcalfe stopped at the Sandwich Islands en route to or from China during 1788, quite likely both.

Such information as exists comes indirectly from the log of John Boit, captain of another ship. Quoting Young, Boit recorded: "It appeared that Captain Metcalfe had purchased his small vessel [*Fair American*] at Macao after his arrival at that port in the *Eleanora* from the Northwest Coast and did then fit her with the snow for the coast again and gave the command of her to his eldest son."[5] The key words here are "after his arrival at that port [Macao]." This bolsters the case for there having been a 1788 voyage after leaving Macao and that it had been to the Northwest Coast.

Further evidence that the *Eleanora* had visited Hawai'i prior to the 1789 visit, when Young was stranded, comes from a 1798 statement related by Young to Captain Ebenezer Townsend. One reason young Thomas Metcalfe met his death at the hands of vengeful Hawaiians in early 1790 was, Young told Townsend, because he "placed too much confidence in the Indians [*sic*], having visited the island before."[6] Thomas Metcalfe could only have visited the island in 1788, when the *Eleanora* made its first trip to the Northwest Coast from Macao.

Records of the East India Company, Canton Factory, note the arrival of the *Eleanora* on August 12, 1788.[7] That arrival could only have been the 1788 return from the Northwest. For the next four months, until December 9, 1788, there was little work for the crew as the vessel lay anchored among other ships, large and small, in Lark's Bay, a few miles south of Macao in the estuary of the Pearl River. In fact, so well under control were matters that Metcalfe was often in Macao enjoying his time away from the ship.

The area that Captains Metcalfe and Colnett had sailed their vessels into was a restless, turbulent port where predators lurked and looked for easy prey. The night of December 9, 1788, found Metcalfe and his sons ashore hobnobbing with other officers and port nabobs. A number of the crew also had shore leave, and John Young may well have been among them. Shortly after twilight a band of brigands fell upon the *Eleanora*, wreaking considerable damage. They sought the gold and silver that they assumed Metcalfe had hidden away, the result of his lucrative sale of seal-skins. After pillaging the ship and finding no coins, the pirates torched the vessel and ransacked what did not burn. When Metcalfe returned he was greeted by the acrid smell of smoke and gunpowder. He also found that an officer and the first mate had been felled by pirate pistols.

It would take many weeks before the racked ship was once again ready for another voyage. And for sure, much of the task of making the vessel shipshape for its next trip fell to its boatswain, John Young. The pirate pillage, more than any other factor, is probably why Metcalfe put off his return journey to the Northwest for more fur trading until early in June of 1789. Another reason Metcalfe may have delayed the trip to America was that he planned to first sail to Russian territory, to the huge Kamchatka peninsula on Siberia's eastern coast. It was a seven-thousand-mile round trip that began on January 24, 1789, for the purpose of obtaining a cargo of Siberian furs. Whether Metcalfe succeeded is unknown, due to the loss of the ship's log. Nonetheless, it was another opportunity for boatswain John Young to learn just how wide a world it was. The trip took two months.

Metcalfe was back in Macao by March 30, the date of a letter he wrote to his son George in Albany, New York. No mention was made of any voyages past or planned. The letter's purpose was primarily to inform his eldest son that he had "remitted a Bill of Exchange for 300 pounds sterling" on a London bank, "and she [Mrs. Metcalfe] and you may draw for a part of the money at 3 months." He devoted a paragraph to the problem with the pirates, pointing out that "your bro. Thom. and others much wounded. [Brother] Robert had a still narrower escape after hanging by the lap of a Sailors Jacket some time in the water [and] recovered a Boat and escaped to Macao. . . . I am too much pressed with business to give any further details of my Voyage. I am, Dr. Geo, your affec. father, Simon Metcalfe."[8]

Very likely some of the pressing business was his purchase of a small schooner, probably from the profits of his Falkland furs. Metcalfe had the schooner, originally designed as a yacht, redesigned to fit his needs as a companion vessel capable of entering and exiting among the many islets, bays, and estuaries that he had found along the Northwest Coast. He renamed it the *Fair American*. Undoubtedly it was with paternal pride that he put his son Thomas, who was then nineteen years old, in command. Five other sailors comprised the total of six men aboard the ship. One of them was Isaac Davis, whom Metcalfe had the good sense to name as first mate. Davis was a seasoned sailor, born in 1756 in Milfordhaven, in the south-western tip of Wales. It cannot be ascertained that he had been a crew member on the *Eleanora,* but it is quite unlikely that Metcalfe would have trusted anyone as a first mate but a sailor in whom he had the utmost confidence. He knew his son was a novice in maritime matters and that none but a steady and experienced hand could be trusted to sail such a small vessel into the tempestuous seas of the north Pacific Ocean. He made a good choice in Isaac Davis.

4 ❧ Who Bought Colnett's Bosun?

Two recent biographers of Simon Metcalfe draw the conclusion that John Young had been in the service of the British Captain James Colnett and while at Macao was lured by Metcalfe's money to take a berth as boatswain on the *Eleanora*. Rhys Richards, author of "Captain Simon Metcalfe, Pioneer Fur Trader," acknowledges reasonable speculation in recounting the voyages of the *Eleanora*, considering that Metcalfe's log was lost at sea. Richards uses literary license but gives it a ring of credibility. On the subject of Metcalfe's bosun, in well-spelled-out factual information, he writes:

In April [1789] Colnett had the misfortune to lose his boatswain, as well as copies of his journals and charts, to the blandishments and dollars of Simon Metcalfe. Since Colnett's stock of charts included all those made by Portlock, Dixon and Meares, as well as the subsequent addition by Colnett and Duncan, Metcalfe felt he had made a real coup to benefit his second voyage to the coast.[1]

Equally convinced that Metcalfe's money won Young over at Macao was Henry G. Despard. So thorough was Despard in his research that he made at least one trip from Michigan to Hawai'i for the purpose of visiting those sites where Metcalfe and his ship had been. Despard's long bibliography is impressive. His references include records from the Maritime Court of the Port of St. Louis on the Island of Mauritius, where Metcalfe once gave testimony as to ports he had touched upon in that part of the globe. Unfortunately, Despard did not live to see his well-polished work published. He died in October 1995.[2]

Those who have read Despard's unpublished manuscript view it as imaginative in parts, yet believable and as historically accurate as possible, judging from the research that is catalogued. Many of the ports and places he cites as having been touched on by the *Eleanora* he drew from reliable records. Like Richards, he uses logical speculation and assumptions in taking Metcalfe and his crew from one part of the world to another. The "log" he presumes Metcalfe kept is convincing and interesting. With regard to John Young, Despard relates:

But as always, secrets will out and Simon Metcalfe [in Macao] was already on the prowl. There was much to be learned from those seamen who had shipped to the Coast, now looking for berths on some new venture such as the Eleanora *had to offer. Among those to sign on with Metcalfe was one John Young, lately bosun of the* Prince of Wales—*for a few more dollars and the promise of change. Simon considered himself fortunate to have secured a boatswain with such experience aboard.*[3]

Despard went to his grave convinced that John Young had earlier been Colnett's boatswain aboard the *Prince of Wales*.

George W. Collins, in his draft of a history of Young and Davis, wrote:

It is my theory that he [Young] signed with Metcalfe in Canton, China, or at Macao, sometime between November 25, 1788, and March 15, 1789, during which interval he had received the balance of moneys due him under articles signed in 1789, in connection with a joint venture the South Seas and East Indies Companies, as employers, operating the two licensed ships, the Prince of Wales *and the* Princess Royal, *commanded by James Colnett for a trading voyage to the Northwest coast of America.*[4]

Having stated that Young was on the *Eleanora* when it left New York in 1787, a look at the other side of the coin, the Colnett side, is warranted. The Devonshire-born James Colnett was a young British midshipman when he sailed with Captain James Cook in September 1771. He was with him when Cook sighted New Caledonia, where Mount Colnett and Cape Colnett on that island bear his name. A cape on the Pacific side of Mexico is also named Colnett.[5] On February 4, 1779, after serving on at least four other British navy ships, he "obtained his standing as a lieutenant in the Royal Navy."[6] He rose through the ranks on various vessels until August 1786, when he was placed on half pay. He sought and received permission from the Royal Admiralty to take command of the *Prince of Wales* and the *Princess Royal* for the purpose of fur trading between the American Northwest and China. That same year the two vessels sailed out of Spithead, England, for their far-flung destination.

Chapter 4

In 1789, when Metcalfe was still in Macao, Captain Colnett transferred to the snow *Argonaut,* also in Macao. His sponsors appear to have been the British East India Company and the South Seas Company, also known as the Nootka Sound Company. The next three years, 1787 to 1789, saw Colnett roaming the channels, islands, inlets, islets, bays, and ocean waters from Nootka Sound (now Vancouver Island) as far north as Unalaska and as far west as Japan. Evidence of that visit is the Colnett Strait located between two small islands off the southern tip of Kyushu. With a ship's cargo of sealskins, he made his way to Macao at least three times. There is evidence that he was in Macao and Canton in 1788 and early 1789, at the same time the *Eleanora* was completing her trading, reprovisioning, and refitting for her long voyage back to the Northwest.

Colnett's journal reflects the shortage of competent seamen and complains that it was necessary to comply with their exorbitant demands. He speaks of three ships in the Macao port, two of which were Metcalfe's *Eleanora* and his recently acquired *Fair American.* In February 1789 he wrote: "Our competitors, fitting out here under Portuguese and American colors, used every effort to get our men, and a few dollars bought our boatswain who had been on a former voyage with me. Many more would have followed had they not been immediately articled [i.e., signed up].[7]

This disclosure has had the effect of convincing interested parties that the boatswain who was seduced by Metcalfe's money was none other than the veteran seaman John Young. Although the "bought bosun" is unnamed by Colnett, it is a fact that Young was the boatswain on the *Eleanora* when it left him in Hawai'i in 1790. There remains also a bit of guilt by association in that Metcalfe's lack of scruples would not have prevented him from winning over another ship's key seaman.

If Young was indeed the boatswain Colnett lost and Metcalfe gained, then Young would have sailed earlier with Colnett. He would have traveled on cold northern waters on the *Prince of Wales* rather than the salubrious seas taken by the *Eleanora* from New York to Macao via Batavia. He would have been with Colnett during the many months the British merchant ship threaded its way among frigid coastal shores, searching for furs from Nootka Sound to Kodiak Island. He would have seen Colnett trading with the Indians of the Queen Charlotte Islands and at a host of other seal and otter-bearing shores off the Northwest Coast, all the way to the Aleutians. Young would have been exposed to trading not only with Haida Indians, but he would have met the Eskimo-Aleuts in the Unalaska region. Perhaps most interesting were the Russian traders who had established their government on Kodiak four years earlier. It is also likely that Young would have encountered Japanese fishermen as a result of Colnett's journey to that closed country.

Whether Young sailed solely with Metcalfe, or earlier with Colnett, may never be made clear, as documentation, such as articles of agreement, is lacking.[8] Richards and Despard are both convinced of the Colnett connection, and Collins, who also did a prodigious amount of research, "leans to the theory" that Colnett lost Young to Metcalfe.[9] In Barnard's recounting of Young's story in 1816, he says only that Young "entered as Boatswain on an American ship, Captain Metcalf [*sic*], who was bound on a trading voyage to the North-West Coast."[10] Young's signing on the *Eleanora* could well have been at Macao or Canton, where both captains were anchored with their ships over a period of months. There is reason to believe that in 1788, or 1789 at the latest, John Young left the services of Colnett and was taken on by Metcalfe as boatswain of the *Eleanora*.

In either case, we have his word for it, as told to Captain Barnard, that he saw the celestial city of Canton. He could have been with either captain at the time. That city, like the Russian Kodiak Island, was a far cry from the landscape of his youth in Great Crosby, where he grew up on his father's two-acre plot of farm land. Regardless of the ships he sailed on, the lad from Lancashire had, by middle age, viewed the world through very wide windows.

5 ❖ Macao to the Northwest

June's fair weather was the signal for Metcalfe and his sons Thomas and Robert to depart China in separate ships for the Northwest Coast of America to purchase more furs to bring back to Canton six months or so later. Early on the morning of June 5, 1789, both the snow *Eleanora* and the schooner *Fair American* departed Lark's Bay under full sail.[1] Once again they chose the northern route, probably to allow them to reach the upper latitudes of the Northwest Coast and then, once in Alaska, sail southward to the lower seal-hunting grounds, to arrive at Nootka Island, the first planned rendezvous.

All went well until the ships were off the southeast coast of the Japanese islands, where a storm of considerable strength blew up. In the buffeting the two vessels became separated. For the rest of the eastbound journey they sailed independently, each unaware of the other's location. By the end of June the *Eleanora* had reached the offshore islands of North America, well above Nootka, the chosen rendezvous. Metcalfe had headed for the fifty-fourth north latitude, which would bring him into Dixon Entrance and the Queen Charlotte Islands.[2] Not until late October did the *Eleanora* sail south for Nootka. Metcalfe had used his time bartering and buying furs to take back to China come year's end.

The Indians with whom they traded for otter skins were less than hospitable, and Metcalfe never let his guard down. On many a visit to a bay or inlet the presence of warriors with spears and daggers told him that a safe distance was his best life insurance. Fresh fish provided the first healthful food the crew had consumed since they had left the Orient. Sometimes meals were eaten on shore in a native gathering. But once, when it was observed that the Indians were sending their women away, Metcalfe sensed trouble and cut short the meal and the visit.

The *Eleanora* continued to sail cautiously south, while ever on its port side were the snow-clad peaks of the upper Rockies. Down their slopes were thick forests, whose shoreline trees provided fuel for the ship's galley. As the autumn weather turned blustery Metcalfe headed for Nootka, where he was to be rejoined with his son Thomas and the *Fair American*.

Thomas had not only managed to survive the storm in the small but seaworthy schooner, but he too had reached the Northwest Coast in midsummer and had sailed as far north as Unalaska, from there idling down the Pacific Coast until late October for the agreed-upon Nootka regrouping and return to China via the Sandwich Islands.

Those plans soon went awry, due largely to the Spaniards who saw Nootka as their upper command base. Everything south along the coast down to Mexico was under the Spanish flag. When the *Fair American* arrived offshore of Nootka, its sails were tattered and torn, rendering the vessel next to helpless. Seeking shelter and a chance to make repairs, Nootka Harbor seemed the best choice. They were not turned away by the Spaniards, who proved friendly and invited young Thomas Metcalfe to seek shelter in a nearby cove. While Nootka Sound was generally well known to the few trading ships that ventured this far north, it was off limits to hostile nations, Great Britain in particular. Americans were considered neutral. But a problem arose when the Spaniards found the young captain unable to produce any papers or registry for himself, his crew, or the *Fair American*. Despite his pleas, young Metcalfe was given no choice but to be escorted by two Spanish vessels to San Blas, the Spanish territorial capital, on the west coast of Mexico, several thousand miles south. Its governor would rule as to the possible impropriety of foreign vessels intruding in Spanish domain.

On the very day of the *Fair American*'s departure from Nootka Sound for San Blas, the *Eleanora* appeared for the rendezvous. It remains unclear whether Simon Metcalfe recognized his schooner in the flotilla leaving the area for the south. The imperious Spanish allowed no opportunity for the *Eleanora* to attempt a rendezvous with its schooner, but instead signaled the brig to enter Nootka Harbor. Sensing a trap, Metcalfe maneuvered his ship and sailed out of range, just as a Spanish cannon fired at it. Distance was on his side and he immediately vacated the area and headed in the opposite direction, toward the Sandwich Islands.

At San Blas, where the *Fair American*'s fate was weighed by the governor, its American identity was confirmed and thus it was deemed neutral and harmless. After finding that the ship was not a threat, the Spanish garrison worried about the expenses that would be incurred in keeping the schooner in its power, and the case was dismissed. In early January 1790 the

Fair American sailed directly west, heading for the next planned rendezvous with the *Eleanora*, Kealakekua Bay, on the west coast of Hawai'i Island, two thousand miles away.

The *Eleanora*, having started its southwest journey around the first of November, soon traded scowling skies for a canopy of blue and seas that slapped happily against the ship's sides. Favored by tradewinds, the *Eleanora* made good time. The crew was relatively relaxed, as relaxed as any crew could be under a taskmaster like Metcalfe. There would be no more cold waters, and there was a promise of fresh fruits, vegetables, and unsalted pork. The crew's recollection of having spent time the previous year, however brief, in these languid islands was a great morale builder.

In early December cumulus clouds on the horizon, often a sign of land below, gave hope that this leg of the journey would soon be at an end. Only a day or so later a sailor high aloft in the rigging broke the monotony by bellowing, "Land ho!" There on the rim of the horizon 150 miles leeward was a blue blimp, the barely discernible Mauna Kea, one of the highest mountains in the Pacific Ocean. In short order its southern sister, Mauna Loa, raised her rounded head. Maui's Haleakalā soon rose on the starboard side as the *Eleanora* made her way to Hilo, sheltered by the green cliffs that ring the Hamakua coast. There is no record that the ship touched at Hilo Bay, then but a small village, but rather it proceeded to its west Hawai'i destination of Kealakekua Bay in a couple of weeks of casual sailing. Wintering in Hawai'i was always a warm and welcome respite, especially to those seamen who had spent months in north Pacific seas.

6 ❧ Massacre on Maui

Many a trading ship's captain, and indeed the crew, were long convinced that the then Sandwich Islands comprised the paradise of the Pacific well before that term became a cliché. A vessel going "to trade" needed only enough provisions to get it to those islands. There they knew they could replenish their larder, then trade well beyond the islands, especially to China, and always return when the need arose.

The Hawaiian Islands were not only a port in a storm, they were a welcome tonic from a monotonous diet of stale water, salted meat, and crackers. The climate surpassed anything they had ever experienced, no matter how many foreign ports at which they had dropped anchor. In general, as the saying goes, the natives were friendly, unless provoked into an altercation, such as that which led to the death of Captain James Cook in 1779. Not to be neglected nor sold short were the charms and caresses of the female species.

It was more than a way station for the *Eleanora* when it touched the shore of leeward Hawai'i Island in December 1789, only a decade after Cook's demise in the same vicinity. It was the second visit to the Sandwich Islands for the *Eleanora*. The previous summer Metcalfe had laid over for refreshing and replenishing off Hawai'i Island, en route to Cathay with furs. That was, it is reckoned, the first visit of an American ship to the island chain. As had been the case in 1788, Metcalfe, the mariner-merchant, again had trade in mind. In addition to carrying furs for the Chinese market, he took on hundreds of piculs of precious sandalwood for the ready and waiting wealthy Chinese.[1] Metcalfe also had leisure time while he awaited the arrival of his son aboard the *Fair American*. It was time well used for making necessary repairs to the ship. Beyond that his search for fresh water was foremost if for no other reason than it would counter and help wash down the salted meats and other viands that made up much of the crew's monotonous diet. Fresh water was scarce on the Kealakekua side of the island, where few springs were found and there flowed no running mountain streams. Maui was only a few leagues northwest, and in late January 1790, the *Eleanora* was gently cruising the leeward shores of that island. Metcalfe knew, perhaps from his stopover one year earlier, that fresh fruits, vegetables, fish, and meat were as available there as water. Trading was in order, and out came the red Bengal cloth, trinkets, nails, and ironware so prized by the Hawaiians. Any metal was coveted. As Cook had learned in Tahiti and Hawai'i, the Polynesian propensity for pilfering was associated with chisels and hatchets, efficient tools for fashioning spears, building canoes and furniture, and carving wooden bowls. It was a great improvement over the basalt adze.

When, on January 30, 1790, the vessel lay off the calm waters of Maui's Ma'alaea Bay, it drew the usual crowd of natives—the curious and the traders. The *Eleanora* cruised a few miles farther and dropped anchor off the little coastal village of Honua'ula. Bartering for limes—a deterrent for the dreaded scurvy—hogs, bananas, coconuts, chickens, sweet potatoes, and taro got underway and would continue the next day as more canoes, filled with Hawaiians eager for foreign cloth and metal, would gather under the ship's side. It was close to midnight when the ship's cutter, which was tied to the stern, was cut free by one or more stealthy Hawaiians who may have used knives made of sharks' teeth or bamboo to sever the line. Their aim was not the boat itself but its precious metal fittings. Sleeping in the stolen cutter was a Filipino watchman named Anthony. When he awoke to find himself being pirated, he was already halfway to shore. As he was about to cry an alarm to the *Eleanora*'s watch, one of his captors plunged a dagger into his body and then decapitated him.

The story of the Olowalu Massacre, which soon followed, has been told and retold. Three sources seem to be the most reliable, credible, and in general agreement on details. One is that of John Young himself, who told his story to Captain George Vancouver four years later.[2] Another credible version comes from Hawaiians in 1839, in an account that Dorothy Kahananui edited and translated.[3] The Hawaiians who told the story would have been children and adolescents of the survivors and even eyewitnesses. The third version, and by far the most complete, is that which appeared in the *Columbian Centinel,* published by Benjamin Russell in Boston. The full story appeared in its issue of November 30, 1791, about eleven months after the event. It is told in the first person, by an unnamed seaman. All three versions have been drawn upon here.

When the watch on the *Eleanora* was alerted of the stolen cutter, a boat was immediately launched in pursuit, but it leaked badly and the rescue had to be abandoned. As for the stolen cutter, it was soon broken up and its metal salvaged. Its nails would be fashioned into strong hooks for ocean fishing. The following morning no canoes came to barter, but in the afternoon, the *Centinel* correspondent reported,

two or three canoes came alongside with presents from the Chief, consisting of hogs and fruit, but they were not accepted. The last that came we ordered away immediately, but they paid little attention to it, until we fired, by order of the Captain, five or six musket shots at them, which killed three or four.[4]

That night another Hawaiian swam from the shore, knife in hand, to pry the exterior copper sheeting from the hull of the ship. He apparently thought that this would cause the ship to sink. Metcalfe fired at him with his pistol but missed the mark. Then some of the crew jumped in the water, subdued the man, and brought him aboard. Metcalfe immediately prepared to have the culprit hanged, and had a rope greased and thrown over the yardarm. The *Centinel* reported: "It was only by the persuasion of Mr. Chambers [presumed to be first mate] and myself, he concluded to save his life and keep him prisoner."

The following day, after being threatened by a considerable number of natives armed with slings, stones, arrows, and spears, the *Eleanora* moved in close to shore and fired grape and round shot at the warriors, "dislodging them from their village. At 12 o'clock I went on the shore with the boat and six men and set fire to village . . . and also fired upon the natives . . . but by the constant firing from the ship they did not attempt to attack us."[5]

Some degree of normalcy returned, and during the next three to four days the water casks were filled and it was time to move on from Honua'ula. About then a canoe approached, whose occupants informed Metcalfe that the cutter had been stolen by a chief who lived in a village (Olowalu) beyond the point. The vessel altered its course, made for the point, and there anchored. The next day one of the local chiefs was allowed on board and convinced Metcalfe that, for a reward, he could produce both the cutter and the boatman, Anthony. For the return of the boat Metcalfe offered him the reward of a musket, a bar of iron, eight cartridges, and a piece of Bengal cloth. The same reward was offered for the boatman.

The unnamed seaman told the *Centinel* that after some false starts the following day,

I armed the boat, and again went toward the shore, where after waiting half an hour, they sent a man, who swam to the boat . . . with the thighs of the

[boatman]. I received them and came on board and showed them to Capt. M. who threw them into the sea. A few minutes afterward the same chief came on board for the reward, it was given, and he was also told that if he brought the boat the reward should be paid . . . for he insisted that it was not hurt.

In short order the chief pulled up to the *Eleanora* and there in the canoe he showed the irked and impatient Metcalfe the keel of the stolen boat. Adding insult to injury, he then claimed the reward that had been promised. Hearing this, an angry Captain Metcalfe announced, "That I will now give, the reward they little expect."[6]

Metcalfe's word was as good as his bond. He carried out his diabolical plan with such precision that the carnage he inflicted on the innocent ranks among the worst of maritime atrocities. Outlining his strategy to his key officers, he would, when a substantial number of canoes were alongside for trading, decoy them to the starboard side of the *Eleanora* and fire upon them with all of the ship's mounted guns.

Related the author of the *Centinel* article: "Mr. Chambers and myself tried to persuade the Captain to entice the three chiefs on board and afterward hang them from the fore yard, in view of the whole island . . . but our persuasions were of no effect, he was fully determined to take the following means of punishing them." The witness then graphically described Metcalfe's plan to gather the canoes on the starboard side. He would then

station one man to each port lanyard, and others down to the guns below decks, whilst others on the quarter deck, stationed at the swivels, and four brass guns and when all were ready, to fire immediately into the canoes, at one command. The guns below decks had in each of them 100 musket balls and 50 landgradge nails. There were seven of the above guns, each containing the like quantity. The four guns on the quarter deck had in them 50 balls each, some of the swivels 20, others ten balls.

As told by the *Centinel:*

Mr. Chambers and myself strongly [again] insisted that the punishment was too severe, and only butchering a number of innocent women and children. But he replied [that] we were only trying to take the ship from him, and that his orders should be obeyed, and immediately ordered every man to his station.

By this time the canoes were filled with Hawaiians of both sexes and all ages ready to barter their limes, meat, vegetables, fowl, and fruit, as had been customary and permitted. By order of the captain, the crew directed the vendors to the starboard side. Metcalfe instructed his eager gunners to fire at the command of the word "Anthony." Those sailors who were Filipino or Portuguese were only too pleased to avenge the death of one of their shipmates. Metcalfe's command soon rang out, followed instantly by a fiery barrage from the ship's guns.

The result was a broadside of musket balls and pointed nails directly into the canoes crowded with young and old of both sexes. Competing with the noise of shell fire that raked the trapped victims were their agonized shrieks of pain and anger. Those cries continued long after the firing and the smoke had subsided. The author of the *Centinel* article wrote:

The horrible scene that ensued is too much for any pen. The water alongside continued of a crimson color for at least ten minutes. Some were sinking, others were, lying half out of their canoes without arms or legs, while others lay in the canoes wettering [sic] *in their own blood."*

The estimates of fatalities range from eighty to more than a hundred. John Young, a witness to the slaughter, told Vancouver that the guns between decks, being on a level with the canoes, "did a great execution, as did the small arms from the quarter deck and other parts of the ship."[7] It was Young's opinion that upward of a hundred were killed. Later reports told of many more dying from their wounds.

When the carnage was concluded, according to Young, "Having taken such revenge as he considered equivalent to the injury received, Mr. Metcalfe quitted Mowee and returned with vessel to Owhyee, where, to all appearance they were on very good terms with the chiefs and the inhabitants of that island."[8] This would have been in early February of 1790.

A bit of irony came to light when it was learned that the Olowalu chief responsible for the theft of the cutter was not among those in the canoes raked with the *Eleanora*'s weapons.

7 ❧ Seizure at Sea

When the *Fair American* left Nootka Sound under escort by two Spanish vessels, it followed the coast of upper California, then sailed past Baja California, until it reached the Spanish headquarters at San Blas, on Mexico's west coast. If the convoy stopped over at the Presidio in San Francisco de Assisi, and also Monterey, for refreshment, as would have been likely, it is not recorded. Both were Spanish military and trading centers. San Blas was another thousand miles to the south, and it was there that the governor of the western region of New Spain held forth. It was he who decided the schooner was not a threat and released it in January 1790.

It remains a mystery as to why the schooner took ten weeks, twice as long as the anticipated time, to reach the Hawaiian Islands, more than two thousand miles distant. Bad weather may have been a factor, for storms in the north Pacific at that time of year send high and dangerous seas to the lower latitudes. Or perhaps after sailing out of San Blas the *Fair American*'s captain, young Thomas Metcalfe, decided to make a friendly visit to the Islas Marias, which lay about seventy-five miles off the coast. In any event, it was early March when the vessel first sighted the Sandwich Islands. With the help of the experienced first mate, Isaac Davis, young Captain Metcalfe maneuvered the ship into the Alenuihāhā channel, between Maui and Hawai'i Island. It was now only one or two days sailing to reach Kealakekua, the second rendezvous agreed upon between father and son.

Here and there, as they sailed close to the north Kohala coast of the Big Island, they encountered an occasional canoe manned by stalwart Hawaiians. Signals and greetings were exchanged in passing. They sailed by the harbor of Kawaihae on March 16, headed for Kealakekua. (This would be the day before John Young was given leave to go ashore at Kealakekua, possibly to inquire of the *Fair American*.) At about eighteen miles west of Kawaihae, they were just off the small village of Ka'ūpūlehu. A canoe approached with at least half a dozen husky Hawaiians, who indicated, by friendly signs, that they wanted to welcome the schooner to the area and wished to come aboard to exchange greetings and gifts and sell hogs and vegetables at next to nothing. Thomas Metcalfe was quite agreeable, as was his crew, with the exception of Isaac Davis. It had been many weeks since they had had dealings with anyone, and the crew welcomed the idea of meeting with friendly visitors.

As Metcalfe arranged for the eager Hawaiians to board, Davis cautioned him; his sixth sense and more mature instincts told him these natives were overly friendly, that they were up to mischief. Nonsense, countered the nineteen-year-old Captain Metcalfe, as he thought of trading some of his skins and artifacts from the Northwest for Hawaiian gifts, and for a change, some fresh fruits and vegetables. As Davis related to Captain George Vancouver in 1793, he thought the "behavior of the natives had a very suspicious appearance, but all he could urge was to no effect; the young commander, perfectly satisfied of their friendly intentions, replied that they would do them no harm, and allowed as many as thought proper to come on board his vessel."[1] This attitude had been observed the year prior, when the *Eleanora* was in Hawaiian waters. John Young related to Captain Ebenezer Townsend that "one reason young Thomas Metcalfe, in the *Fair American*, was decoyed to his death in Hawai'i was because he placed too much confidence in the Indians [*sic*]."[2]

Thomas saw that a man who appeared to be a chief in the canoe held up a feathered cap, indicating it as a gift. Metcalfe would have had no way of knowing that this was Chief Kame'eiamoku, who had only a short time before been humiliated by a rope lashing at the hands of Simon Metcalfe on the *Eleanora*.[3] This was the same chief who had vowed vengeance in his assertion that he would, at the first opportunity, seize the next visiting vessel that came his way. Little did the chief reckon that his wrath would be taken out on the very son of the man who had humiliated him, and that the vessel he had targeted was the property of Simon Metcalfe.

Once the warriors were allowed to board the schooner, little time was wasted with greetings on the part of the twelve warriors, who were twice the number of the *Fair American*'s crew. As described by Captain Joseph Ingraham, who heard it indirectly from Isaac Davis:

One of the chiefs coming aft with a feathered cap presented it to Captain Metcalf [sic], and at the same time desired he might fit it on his head. In doing which, finding him off his guard, he clasped him round and threw him overboard. At the same instant everyone on board was seized and overpowered by numbers. After being thrown in the sea those in the canoe, in a most cruel manner, beat and bruised them with their paddles, etc. til they put a period to their existence.[4]

Before being thrown into the sea, Davis, who carried a pistol, aimed it at the chief, but it misfired. In seconds "he was seized, thrown overboard and no more was seen."[5] But he did not drown. The first mate was a seasoned sailor, of an athletic build, and apparently, unlike the rest of the crew, an able swimmer. With long and strong strokes he made for one of the canoes. He was mercilessly beaten with paddles, stripped of his clothes by the women, and then "held with his throat across the rafter that unites the two canoes, whilst the inhuman wretches jumped upon his neck and shoulders, with the intention of thus depriving him of his life, but still without effect; till, being tired with their cruelties they ceased to persecute him."[6]

Bleeding and beaten, Davis made his way to another canoe, and,

looking up at the most active of the party, said, "mytie, mytie," signifying "good"; the man instantly replied "arrowha" [aloha], meaning that he pitied him, and . . . by touching noses gave him some cloth, and assisted him to wipe and bind up his wounds. After this he had no other injury offered to him; on his being taken on shore he was kindly treated by Harapy, brother to Kahowmotoo [Keʻeamoku], who nursed him; and expressed great concern for his deplorable condition; but Tamahamootoo [Kameʻeiamoku] not withstanding the state he was in, took him in triumph through the village, and made a jest of him.[7]

It was far more than an act of piracy, and it was over in a matter of minutes. The object was not gold and spices, but sweet revenge. The booty was the *Fair American* and the lone survivor was Isaac Davis. According to Hawaiiana historian Terry Wallace, the booty included, besides seal and/or otter skins, a number of muskets, pistols, and swivel guns, and three small brass cannons.[8] At least one of these, named Lopaka, for Robert, would contribute to Kamehameha's future conquests.

Kamehameha was quite chagrined when he learned of the theft of Metcalfe's schooner, which he felt should be returned to its owner. Vancouver relates:

*The attack
on the* Fair
American *off
the west coast of
Hawaiʻi Island,
March 1790.*
© *Herb Kawainui
Kāne. Collection of
Kona Village Resort*

On the 22nd of March Kamehameha I and Young set out for where the schooner was, and he severely reprimanded Kameeiamoku for his breach of hospitality and inhumanity, and ordered the schooner to be delivered up to him in order to be restored to the owner. Kamehameha also took the wounded Davis under his special care and as a companion to Young.[9]

The roles of the vessel and of Davis, the sole survivor, were still to be played out.[10] The involvement of John Young and Davis with King Kamehameha would soon bring a new and lasting direction to Hawai'i's history.

8 ❧ Detained or Kidnapped?

The morning of March 16, 1790, with its clear skies, calm seas, and soft breezes, was typical weather for the Kona coast of Hawai'i. The *Eleanora* continued its task of loading sandalwood from the Kealakekua shore. A few more days and it could sail for the return trip to China. But Simon Metcalfe chafed as the expected rendezvous with the *Fair American* failed to materialize. It was a quirk of fate that the schooner, only about forty miles to the northeast, never appeared. Had Thomas elected to sail on to Kealakekua instead of tarrying to trade with the canoe off Ka'ūpūlehu, the two ships would have been joined on this day.

The next day, March 17, marked John Young's forty-sixth birthday. Since the ship was safely anchored, Young knew he could be spared and asked for leave to go ashore to hunt birds. Metcalfe granted overnight leave and probably asked Young to make inquiry with regard to the missing *Fair American*, knowing that there were four white men on shore and hoping they could provide some answers.

Word of the *Fair American*'s disastrous end had already reached Kealakekua and the ears of Kamehameha and his chiefs. They had probably also been informed of the recent massacre at Olowalu. Kamehameha knew that to prevent a similar slaughter from the guns of the *Eleanora* at Kealakekua not an inkling of the *Fair American*'s fate should reach the vindictive Simon Metcalfe. He feared that the captain's revenge for the murder of his son and the loss of his schooner would make the Olowalu Massacre seem like a minor fracas. Kamehameha immediately imposed a *kapu* forbidding every canoe in the area from putting to sea. The same applied to any individuals who might wish to swim to the vessel. A violation of the *kapu* could bring death by strangling.

A quarter of a century later, John Young related to Captain Charles Barnard the circumstances that brought him to Hawai'i, and in particular, the events of the day he found himself stranded. Barnard became acquainted with Young in 1816 when he asked Kamehameha for permission to obtain sandalwood. The king told him that all business matters were left to John Young. Barnard and Young met, a deal was made to obtain the cargo, and it was then that Barnard, during their leisure time while cargo was being carried and loaded, drew from Young the story of his arrival in Hawai'i. In his autobiography, Barnard wrote:

John Young . . . is the oldest white settler on the island; he had been sent for by the king, who reposes great confidence in him, in conducting and concluding bargains with the whites, and for that intent the king had sent him on board; so it now rested pretty much with him whether we should procure sandalwood or not.[1]

The captain was successful in getting the desired cargo and describes Young piloting his vessel, the *Hope,* to the area for loading the sandalwood. "The natives were yet engaged," wrote Barnard,

in bringing it upon their backs from the surrounding mountains to the place of deposit, which was near the dwelling of John Young, who weighed and delivered it. As it did not arrive so fast as to keep us constantly employed, I used to converse with Young in these intermissions.

Barnard relates that Young was agreeable to spinning yarns and that Young said to him, "As we are now at leisure I will relate to you some of the events that had, so unexpectedly, and against my inclination, caused me to become an inhabitant of Owyhee." Barnard wrote: "I listened to my companion with the greatest degree of interest, and he accordingly communicated to me the following train of adventures." What follows is like the scriptural tale of Esau and Jacob: that is, the story is of John Young, but the words are of Barnard. There are other versions of this story, but this is Young's account as told by Captain Barnard in 1816. In his book Barnard titles this chapter "The Narrative," told in the first person by Young, who begins:

Tired of being constantly on board, I one day [March 17, 1790], took a musket and went on shore, intending to take a ramble through the woods in pursuit of birds. In the middle of the afternoon, I returned to the shore, for the purpose of going on board, but there was no boat and all the canoes were hauled higher up on the beach as usual; the huts were all closed, and not a native visible. I felt a strange kind of fear creeping over me at this unusual state of things. All was still and gloomy as death; I traveled the lonely beach back and forth with hurried steps, with my eye directed to the ship, with the hope of seeing a boat put off from her, to come to my relief. Night set in and everything was wrapped in uncertainty.

Young then approached, with fear, one of the huts and knocked, wondering as he waited if he would be offered up as a sacrifice, "but commended myself to Providence." After knocking again, he was invited to enter and refreshments were offered to him. He discerned by the countenance of his hosts that something dreadful had happened, "but of what nature it was, or who were the victims of it, I could not, from my ignorance of the language, ascertain." He said that during the long night he never closed his eyes, tossing and turning, and in his dreams imagined a dire end. Even his clothes, which were hung in the room, assumed the aspect of some "deadly assassin venturing to steal upon my defenseless position, and send me into a world of spirits, without a witness to declare the author."

When morning finally came, Young hastened to the beach, gazing intently at the *Eleanora*. But no boat or signal came from her, and the canoes remained high and dry on the shore. Feeling sick and faint, and completely discouraged, he returned to the grass house, where he was entreated to eat. He related that his appetite had disappeared with his spirit. He observed that an appearance of concern was seen on the countenance of the natives, and continued: "This confirmed my suspicions that some serious occurrence had taken place, but of what nature I could not even conjecture. The day closed without anything taking place in my favor and was followed by a wretched and sleepless night . . . worse than the last." The next morning he again went to the shore and fixed his attention on the *Eleanora*, where he observed the crew carrying out their duties,

but to my consternation no boat came from her for me. At length she got under weigh [about March 24] and continued standing in and out . . . but who can describe or even conceive my feelings when I first saw the ship bear off, and rig out her steering-sail booms. This sight overpowered me; I felt deprived of emotion, and almost out of sense, imagining that the hour of death had come.

The lonely sailor was in despair for the next two days and could remember very little of what occurred. Following the departure of his ship, his only home, he noticed that things had seemingly returned to normal and the natives "resumed their usual occupations." He took heart only when a Hawaiian made signs to him that there was another white man in the vicinity and he would guide him to this man if he wished: "I set off in company with the Indian [*sic*], and it was a source of comfort to me that I was now likely to meet with a sympathizing friend to whom I could communicate my sorrows."

Upon arriving at the Hawaiian village of Kailua, Young found that the man was Isaac Davis, one of those who had been aboard the *Fair American*. Quite likely he and Young had earlier been shipmates aboard the *Eleanora*. He was, Young said, "confined to the hut by numerous wounds inflicted by knives and daggers and bruises from clubs. I was alarmed at seeing Davis in this suffering and destitute state, but yet hopes were entertained that his case was not dangerous."

Barnard's version differs somewhat from the one that Captain George Vancouver heard from Young in 1793, twenty-three years earlier. Young told Vancouver that he had permission to remain onshore overnight, which is contrary to his telling Barnard of his attempt to return to the brig at the end of his day of hunting birds. Moreover, Young must have first met Kamehameha as Young was about to return to his ship, for as Vancouver heard it,

the snow stood close in, and fired a gun as a signal for him to return on board; but to his very great astonishment he found all the canoes tabooed, and hauled up on the shore, and was informed by Tamaahmaah [Kamehameha], that if he attempted to take a canoe by himself, he would be put to death, but that he should have a canoe the very next day.[2]

Young submitted, and that evening he learned with surprise of the fate of the *Fair American*:

The snow remained two days off Karakakooa [Kealakekua] firing guns and standing in shore, as a signal for Young; but after the news was confirmed of the schooner having been captured the king would not permit him to leave the island, but behaved to him in the kindest manner; telling him he should not be hurt, and that he should be at liberty to depart in the next ship that arrived; but that he would, on no account, allow a canoe to get off the snow, lest all the people be killed.[3]

Abraham Fornander agrees that Kamehameha could not risk Metcalfe learning the fate of his son and his schooner, and he also says that "Kamehameha having obtained a quantity of arms and ammunition, was anxious of having a foreigner . . . who knew how to use them and keep them in order."[4]

According to Vancouver, Kamehameha, "who had [earlier] been on the friendliest terms with Mr. Metcalfe,"[5] took Young to his own house and treated him with attention and kindness. As for the capture of the schooner, the king expressed indignation at the perpetrators for the attack and set out, accompanied by Young, on March 22, to inquire into the circumstances that caused so great a breach of hospitality.

Vancouver writes that Young and Kamehameha found Davis, sorely wounded, and that the king ordered that Davis be taken to his own house, "and gave particular instructions that he [Davis] should receive every assistance in their power to bestow." Davis later related to Vancouver that he had been treated by the king and his attendants with a degree of kindness and attention that "I could not have believed these people were capable of showing."[6]

Young and Davis had much in common, not only as veteran sailors on the high seas, but in their origins. Young's Lancashire home was only 170 miles from Davis's birthplace of Milford in southwest Wales. Davis was about eight years Young's junior when he was tapped for the role of first mate on the *Fair American*. Presumably, as he was thought to have been the ship's carpenter on Metcalfe's vessel, he had been apprenticed earlier to a shipbuilder in Wales or Liverpool.

Who rescued Davis remains uncertain, but he was brought ashore and nursed back to life, though he was temporarily blinded for several weeks. Kamehameha is credited for having had the wounded foreigner cared for. The king may well have looked upon this seaman as worth saving, a foreigner whose skills might well be put to good use. Davis was far from recovered when John Young was brought to him, quite clearly by order of the king himself.

This would not have been the first time the king had encountered Young. More than once, on earlier occasions, Kamehameha had been aboard the *Eleanora* for purposes of bartering and seeing precious sandalwood loaded. Then he would have observed the boatswain giving orders and taken note of his efficient command of the crew. He may have sized up Young as a man who could prove an asset in his conquest of the islands. Fornander states that when the *Eleanora* was in Kealakekua Bay Kamehameha was "driving a very lucrative trade with . . . Metcalfe and meditating on how to kidnap Metcalfe's boatswain, John Young."[7]

Fate played into Kamehameha's hands when Young took shore leave, then missed his ship by the king's design. The *kapu* ordered by Kame-

Clarion off O'Whyhe 22 March
1790

Sir

As my Boatswain landed by
your _____ if he is not returned to
the Vessel in consequence of an unpleasant
nature now _____ to distress a Vessel in
these Seas is an affair of no small
magnitude if your Word be the
Law of O'Whyhe as you have _____ _____
told me there can be no difficulty in
doing me justice in this _____ _____
I am possessed of sufficient powers to take
ample revenge which it is your duty
to make the head Chief acquainted with

I am Gentlemen

Yours &c

Simon Metcalfe

To
Mess.
C. S. Thomas
J. Adler
T. Mackey
John Young

hameha had shut down everything, including Young's return to the ship he had sailed upon for at least the last two years. On March 22, 1790, Metcalfe sent a threatening letter ashore, addressed to S. I. Thomas, I. Ridler, Jos. Mackey, and John Young, hoping it would produce his sorely needed boatswain.[8] In the upper-right-hand corner he entered "*Eleanora* off Owhyhee 22 March 1790." He then wrote:

As my Boatswain landed by your invitation, if he is not returned to the Vessel, consequences of an unpleasant nature may follow (to distress a vessel in these Seas is an affair of no small magnitude). If your Word be the Law of Owhyhee as you have repeatedly told me, there can be no difficulty in doing me justice in this Business, otherwise I am possessed of sufficient powers to take ample revenge which it is your duty to make the head Chief acquainted with.

I am Gentlemen

Yours &c &c.

[Signed] Simon Metcalfe

When Metcalfe finally sailed off after waiting several days for Young's appearance, he had despaired of rendezvousing with his son and he quite understandably reckoned that his boatswain had been taken prisoner and even executed. The decision was made to weigh anchor and point for China.

Metcalfe's letter poses some interesting questions. While Young told Barnard he went ashore to shoot birds, Metcalfe clearly states that Young "landed by your invitation." Had this quartet invited Young, whom they probably had met at an earlier date, if not on an earlier voyage? Young's statement is contrary to the belief that Metcalfe had sent him ashore to get word of the *Fair American* and his son, which is quite believable.

The four men to whom the letter was directed were not known as beachcombers. Many of the early settlers (and there were few indeed in 1790) were considered "fine, sturdy, upright characters. Some may have been agents for their ship or its owner, with instructions to obtain cargo, do some trading and even learn the language."[9] Metcalfe obviously knew them, and it is not unlikely that they had visited the *Eleanora* earlier and struck up an acquaintance with the captain. Perhaps they were involved with the acquisition and loading of sandalwood.

S. I. Thomas may have been one of the Americans living at Kailua at the time. He arrived there either on the *Columbia* or the *Lady Washington* in about 1788. Isaac Ridler had been the carpenter's mate on the *Columbia*,

A dejected John Young watches the Eleanora
sail off to the Orient without him, March 1790.

Illustration by Herb Kawainui Kāne. Collection of the author

and in 1788 had been left in Hawai'i to gather sandalwood. He lived in Hawai'i for about four years. Mackey was Irish-born and had been in Bombay with the East India Company. He is listed as having been a surgeon with Captain Cook.[10]

The fourth of the addressees is John Young, and to those who believe it was Metcalfe's boatswain this presents an enigma. The use of the name in the letter has somewhat muddied the waters, since it is unlikely that Metcalfe would have addressed a letter to the man whose return he was seeking. This gives rise to the belief that there was more than one John Young in the area, which is not an unreasonable presumption considering the commonalty of both the given and the family name. According to Bruce Cartwright, Jr., "By a strange coincidence the name of one of the Americans residing at Kailua was also John Young, he being the same man that Ingraham picked up off Maui together with I. Ridler and James Cox."[11] It is not known how long this John Young lived in Hawai'i, but it is established that the following year he sailed to China under Captain Joseph Ingraham on the brigantine *Hope*.[12] However, Metcalfe may have directed the letter to his boatswain to make sure he was informed of the situation.

Surely Metcalfe was acquainted with the four men inasmuch as he wrote that his boatswain had gone ashore "by your invitation," which does not agree with Young's statement that he had gone ashore to shoot birds. Also mystifying is Metcalfe's assertion that the four men had repeatedly said that their "Word be the Law." Where did that leave Kamehameha, who surely would have had a contrary view? Metcalfe must be referring to Kamehameha when he mentions "the head Chief."

Clearly the letter, and its threat of dire consequences, had no effect. One reason no reply came from the shore is because of the *kapu* on all canoes. That the letter came to be preserved all those years, presumably by John Young (the Englishman), is remarkable.

Both Young and Davis responded to Kamehameha's kindness and accepted the reality that it could be a long time before another vessel would appear and they would be allowed to depart. A failed opportunity to escape came in 1791. Meanwhile the two stranded, if not kidnapped, British seamen, accepted their present destiny, which included hospitality from as well as service to "the head Chief."

Louis Choris, artist on the Russian ship *Rurick*, wrote a brief account of Young's experience as he heard it from Young. See Appendix I.

9 ❧ King of Kings

Western ways had not yet come to Hawai'i when Kamehameha the Great was born sometime in the middle of the eighteenth century. The Hawaiians did not keep weeks of seven days, though they did keep twelve months, each of thirty days, according to lunar and solar cycles. All information about Kamehameha's birth that is available comes from observers of that period, some who knew him well. Documented Western contact was first made in 1778 by Captain James Cook, the famed British navigator whose skills have seldom been duplicated. The Hawaiian way of calculating time continued well past 1820, when the first company of American missionaries arrived in Hawai'i.[1] Their New England ways brought the Western method of ciphering to reading and measuring time, weight, and distance.

Historians are divided by as many as twenty-four years in determining the date of the future king's birth. On the one extreme, the early Hawaiian historian Samuel M. Kamakau gives 1736, which would have made Kamehameha eighty-two at the time of his death in 1819.[2] But Kamakau's date has been questioned, as have several of his other dates. At the other end of the time spectrum is the date given by the early Spanish resident Francisco de Paula Marin, who knew Kamehameha. Though not a physician, he was called upon because of his medical knowledge to treat the dying monarch in 1819. Marin gives 1758 as the likely birth date. John Young, who from his arrival in 1790 spent much of his time in Kamehameha's company and was at his death bed, estimated that the king was about seventy when he died, which would place his birth at 1749.[3]

Another respected historian, John F. G. Stokes, estimates that the king was born between 1750 and 1760, "probably after 1755."[4] Of considerable interest is information from Dr. Maud Makemson, onetime assistant professor of astronomy at Vassar College. She cites a legend from one Kanalu "relating to the appearance of a new or unusual heavenly body on the night preceding Kamehameha's birth."[5] Halley's comet appeared in 1758, the same year that Marin gives for the year of Kamehameha's birth. That coincides with Marin's date of 1758.

A longtime librarian of the Hawai'i State Archives, Alfred P. Taylor, in his book *Under Hawaiian Skies,* believes the year 1753 is as close an accurate date for the king's birth as can be established. This is midway between the Marin and Young estimates. It is also the date accepted by Dr. Ralph S. Kuykendall, eminent historian of Hawaiiana. It is reasonable, therefore, for this biography to proceed with the premise that Kamehameha was born in 1753. It may well be that a new or unusual heavenly body was seen on the night preceding Kamehameha's birth, but the next night was not fair. Legend has it that lightning and thunder filled the skies that night, bringing rain and stormy seas to the North Kohala coast of Hawai'i Island, the site generally accepted as Kamehameha's birthplace.[6]

Kamehameha's father was the chief Keōua-kupu-a-pa-i-ka-lani, and his mother, also descended from a line of chiefs, was Keku'iapoiwa. The legend goes that the child, born to be a chief, was deemed a threat to Alapa'i, who was chief of the entire island. When he heard of the birth, Alapa'i vowed that there would be no usurper to take away his power, and that he would have a search made for the child and remove the gathering cloud before it was a week old. Happily, Kamehameha's mother was warned of Alapa'i's threat and had her baby spirited away under the cover of darkness to remote 'Āwini Valley on the wild windward shore of the northeast Kohala coast.

Alapa'i had his searchers cover the broad plain and deep mountains of the Kohala district, but their weeks of effort were fruitless. 'Āwini, remote and generally inaccessible, remained the child's home for the first five years of his life, where he had few companions.[7] He had been named Paiea, after the hard-shelled crab, and in his adult life he proved to be tenacious as a crab, fighting hard for every foot of land he won. Because he lived his first years in isolation, he came to be known as Kamehameha, "the lonely one" or "the solitary one."

When he was about five, it was safe for him to return to his Kohala home. It was ordained that he should be schooled not only in the spiritual life of his race but also in the art of warfare. At that time Hawai'i was ruled by numerous high chiefs who not only guarded their terrain well but coveted and fought for the good lands neighboring districts offered. Battle skills were essential to a young chief, and Kamehameha was fortunate to have for his tutor the renowned warrior Kekūhaupi'o.[8]

A more competent trainer could not have been found. Not only did Kamehameha learn the rules of warfare and the art of combat, but he also became adept at such sports and games of skill as wrestling and surfing. He learned to throw and catch spears both defensively and offensively. He had a body built for a king—well proportioned, with a strong physique and a robust body that would serve him equally well in battle and in sports competitions. Even in his adult years, Westerners admired this Atlas-like male who stood well over six feet tall. Foreigners such as Lieutenant James King aboard Cook's vessel thought he had as savage a visage "as I ever saw . . . it however by no means seemed an emblem of his disposition which was good natured & humorous."[9] But the Hawaiian John Papa Ii described Kamehameha and his brother Kalaimamahu as "the handsomest men of those days."[10]

Not neglected in Kamehameha's education were teachings of things sacred and secular, the customs of his people, and chants that recited past achievements, the genealogy of his ancestors, and prayers to Polynesian gods. Rituals of his forefathers, the role of the *kahuna,* the observance of strict *kapu,* sacred ceremonies—all were parts of his early years, and he would adhere to them faithfully until the last hours of his life.[11]

As Kamehameha entered manhood, and Alapaʻi joined his ancestors, Kamehameha gained not only in stature but also in wisdom. So well developed and combined were these features that not only was Kamehameha the most outstanding of all chiefs, but "we can, perhaps, go even further and say that he was one of the great men of the world."[12] Kamehameha was also seen as "an excellent judge of men, [who] had to an unusual degree, the faculty of inspiring loyalty in his followers."[13] Other biographers, such as Gavan Daws, observed that not only was he possessed of a great body, but he was also fearless, brave, and agile.

His supple body was accompanied by a mind that was acute and active. His curiosity contributed to his wisdom, and his wisdom later contributed to his skills as an administrator and an effective organizer. This keen and inquisitive mind also added to his reputation among Westerners as a sharp bargainer and trader. His curiosity would serve him well as he observed Western ways, adapting to those that were to his gain. He had the facility for absorbing new ideas and never lost an opportunity to use them.

Ebenezer Townsend, owner of the ship *Neptune,* wrote an account that attests to Kamehameha's curiosity. Townsend invited Kamehameha aboard his ship when the king was about forty and observed that he became "very active and was all over the ship in a few minutes and making many questions."[14] Townsend showed Kamehameha his compass, hoping to teach him its purpose, but he says he regretted this, "for he kept me at it continually until he learned it."[15]

This curiosity and grasp of foreign ways took firm root with the

Chapter 9

arrival in 1778 of Captain Cook. Kamehameha was about twenty-five years old at the time of Cook's appearance. His uncle, Kalaniopuu, was the high chief of Hawai'i Island and was no longer a young man. On November 30, 1778, Cook's HMS *Resolution,* accompanied by the HMS *Discovery,* was sighted off the southeast coast of Maui, where Kalaniopuu and some of his chiefs were engaged in a battle. These were the first Western vessels the Hawaiians had ever seen, and it was worth halting their war to learn more about these floating islands with big white trees. The chief and a number of his followers went in their canoes to greet the ships, bringing with them gifts of three small pigs and fruit. In his journal for November 10, Cook wrote, "After a stay of about two hours they all left us except six or eight who chused [*sic*] to remain, a double sailing canoe came soon after to attend upon them which we towed a stern all night."[16]

It is generally agreed upon in Hawaiian versions of this story that Kamehameha was among the chiefs who "chused" to remain on board. Abraham Fornander, in his *Account of the Polynesian Race,* reported that when Kamehameha did not return to the shore that night "a great wailing was set up by Kalaniopuu and his retinue, thinking that Kamehameha had been abducted by the ship . . . and their joy was proportionately great when he returned the next day."[17]

An earlier account appeared in 1838, in *Ka Mooolelo Hawaii,* a publication of the Lahainaluna School Press:

Then Kamehameha sailed out and boarded the vessel [off Maui]. When evening came the vessel disappeared over the horizon and Kamehameha slept on board that night. The people thought that Kamehameha had been taken to a foreign land. The people grieved for Kamehameha and they and Kalaniopuu wept. . . . The next morning the vessel returned with Kamehameha on board. He came ashore and the vessel disappeared again, on that disappearance it sailed to Hawaii [Island].[18]

Kamakau's version differs in that he reports that Kamehameha remained on the ship instead of coming ashore the next morning: "But Captain Cook had no intention of carrying them away; he only wanted him to guide them to a good harbor on Hawaii."[19] Cook returned Kamehameha and his companions to Maui, then proceeded to Hawai'i Island. He spent six weeks sailing down Hawai'i's east coast, touching at various bays and inlets. At each place the ship stopped it was greeted by a friendly and astonished audience who came to see the strange sights. The ship sailed to Hilo, a large population center on the windward side of the island, but Cook considered the waters in the bay too stormy to land. By January 17, 1779, the two vessels lay in Kealakekua Bay on Hawai'i's Kona coast. It was by far the best harbor on the island, and it had been home to the young Kamehameha, who had frequently canoed, sailed, swum, and surfed in its waters.

When Kamehameha met Cook and his crew for the first time off Maui, he little knew that he was in the company of a trio of English mariners who, like himself, would each make history within a span of twenty years. Cook would be killed in a historic event within two months. The ship's master, William Bligh, was a witness to his commander's death. A decade later he would be cast adrift by the *Bounty*'s mutineers in a rowboat, only to survive an incredible voyage of nearly four thousand miles from the Tongan islands to the Dutch-held island of Timor. Also on the ship was a young midshipman, George Vancouver, who would later return to Hawai'i and become famous as a superb navigator and explorer.

Captain George Vancouver, who came to know Kamehameha quite well by 1794, had lavish admiration for the chief, considering him the most capable of all chiefs he had met. He viewed Kamehameha as a chief possessed with the qualifications of leadership necessary for the unification of the eight major islands. The friendship between the two deepened with each of the three visits Vancouver made to the archipelago during the early 1790s. Kamehameha may have met Vancouver, and possibly Bligh, when the king, Kalaniopuu, had a formal meeting on board the *Resolution*. Lieutenant King, who had commented on Kamehameha's "savage" appearance, observed that "his manner shewd somewhat of an overbearing spirit, & he seemed to be the principal director in this interview."[20]

Cook's death on February 14, 1779, grew out of a fracas that germinated when it was discovered that a cutter had been stolen during the night, the same situation that provoked the aforementioned massacre at Olowalu more than a decade later. Cook was so annoyed and determined to regain the cutter that instead of dispatching a detachment of men under one of his officers, he personally led his men ashore. Kalaniopuu had returned from Maui only a few days earlier, and Cook attempted to lure the chief on board the ship to be held there as hostage, a ploy that failed. While the Hawaiians were preventing Kalaniopuu from being led to the shore, a shot was fired by a trigger-happy British marine. From then on the affray became blurred and bloody as clubs swung and muskets fired. Cook was in the middle of it when he was struck on the head by one warrior and stabbed by another. The captain fell into a pool and was held there to drown. Kamehameha would surely have been among the bystanders at the beach; he may have been among those who sought to prevent Cook from taking his uncle hostage.

Before peace came a week or so later, there were taunts and threats from both sides. When Captain Charles Clerke saw a Hawaiian twirling Cook's tricornered hat as if in defiance, he ordered four pounders and muskets fired at the Hawaiians. Some were killed, and Kamehameha was wounded in the leg.[21] It was here that he saw for the first time the power and destruction caused by the fire sticks and the larger red-mouthed guns. He learned that such power would determine the outcome of battles, and he was determined from that point on that the weaponry of the foreigners become his ally. Cook's death brought no joy to Kalaniopuu: "The chief [Kalaniopuu] sorrowed over the death of the captain. He dedicated the body of Captain Cook, that is, he offered it as sacrifice to the god with a prayer to grant life to the chief (himself) and to his domain."[22]

Peace came a week later, and a *kapu* was placed on the bay while funeral services were held. Lieutenant King wrote that "many chiefs came on board, who shew'd both a great sorrow for what had happen'd as well as great pleasure that we were friends—Maiha maiha [Kamehameha] & others, who perhaps were afraid of venturing themselves, sent large hogs as peace offerings."[23]

The Cook expedition rent the fabric of Hawai'i's social and political garment, and it could never be repaired. The tear would grow larger in the coming years, as foreign ships and traders, with new customs and old diseases, found their way to the newly-named Sandwich Islands. It was the white man's diseases, first brought to Hawai'i by Cook's crew, that decimated the Hawaiian population by tens of thousands.

While the British expedition was departing Hawai'i in late February for the last time, British troops half a world away were busy in a war against their American colonists, who were attempting to shed the shackles binding them to King George III. Big battles and small skirmishes kept the English and the rebels heavily engaged. Battles and skirmishes of a lesser degree, and with more primitive weapons, were also being waged in Hawai'i by native chiefs. When bigger battles became a reality, it was Kamehameha who was at their forefront, and it was all part of his plan to unite the islands.

Partly because of his subsequent unification of the archipelago, the king has been called the Napoleon of the Pacific by later writers. It is an inapplicable appellation, as he had no dreams of conquest beyond his own horizon. This is not to say that he was uninformed of lands and people in distant places. In the last half of his life he entered into trading with ships from other nations and, with Young as an interpreter, often enjoyed conversing with the vessels' captains. The captains of visiting ships learned from their colleagues that Young was the man to initiate business with, but it was Kamehameha who made the final decisions, and in this he demonstrated common good sense. The Russian naval officer Vasili Mikhailovich Golovnin wrote: "None of the foreigners visiting his country enjoy any exclusive privileges, but all can trade with his subjects with equal freedom. There were those who detected in the king a Yankee shrewdness."[24]

Kamehameha was not unaware that foreign contact would bring serious social change, and he was well aware that there were foreign powers waiting to sweep up his islands for their very own. His awareness of these matters came from visits to ship captains aboard their vessels, or from the captains visiting the royal residence. It was Young who became aware that the visitors' rum, generously served, was not serving his chief well—the king was drinking to excess. The chiefs later blamed the foreigners for bringing the intoxicating beverages. As W. D. Westervelt reported: "Although at first Kamehameha indulged to excess, he was soon convinced by John Young and had the strength of mind to restrict himself to a very small, fixed quantity and finally to abstain from it entirely."[25]

Before the aging Kalaniopuu died, he convened a gathering of his *alii* in remote Waipi'o Valley.[26] His main concern was to see that authority was designated to those who could carry on after his demise. His oldest son, Kiwala'ō, he named as his successor to rule Hawai'i Island. It was to his nephew, Kamehameha, that he gave custody of the image of the war god Kūkā'ilimoku, "the ferocious head of yellow feathers with its staring mother-of-pearl eyes and grinning mouth set with sharks' teeth."[27] Ku was the legendary war god of Hawai'i's kings. Years later Kamehameha would call upon Ku to bring him success in consolidating his conquests.

After the old chief's death, Kiwala'ō did not live long enough to carry the mantle of sovereignty conveyed to him by his father. He was killed in 1782 by one of Kamehameha's chiefs in a fierce and decisive battle at Moku'ōhai in west Hawai'i. Control of Hawai'i Island then fell upon three chiefs, with three divisions. To Keōua (a cousin of Kamehameha) went the southern and lower easterly section of the island, more specifically the Ka'ū district and part of Puna. To the chief Keawemauhili went the other part of Puna, the Hilo district, and parts of the Hamakua district. Kamehameha was ruler of the northern portion of Hamakua, all of Kohala to the north, and Kona on the west side.

Warfare took no holiday as each of the warrior-chiefs sought the lands and power of the others; but in the midst of war there were incidents that led to something more humane than war. In one skirmish south of Hilo Bay, on the lava shore of the Puna coast, Kamehameha jumped from his canoe to pursue two fishermen. In the chase his foot caught in a lava crevice, preventing him from further chase. One of the fishermen seeing his plight turned back and with his paddle struck Kamehameha on the head with such force as to splinter the paddle. Years later the king commemorated this incident by proclaiming *Mamalahoe Kanawai,* known today as the Law of the Splintered Paddle. Its purpose was to shield the helpless and innocent from attacks such as he had received.

During the next four years, Kamehameha was busy protecting his own turf, at the same time seeking to add to it that of the two other Hawai'i Island high chiefs, as they did his lands. He made an unsuccessful invasion in the Hāna district of Maui and a less-than-successful attempt to seize the Hilo district. (It is worth noting that Kamehameha's favorite wife, Ka'ahumanu, was born in Hāna and was renowned for her beauty and high rank.) He later returned to east Hawai'i for another tribal battle and became the victor. Meanwhile, a tenuous peace prevailed among the three chiefdoms in late 1786, and it continued for about five years.

But in 1790 all was not well on the island of Maui, and word of the Maui massacre at Olowalu soon reached Kamehameha. No sooner had the *Eleanora* dropped anchor at Kealakekua Bay, than the chief was told of the Hawaiians' capture of the *Fair American* and the murder of all five members except for its first mate.

Kamehameha now had a very serious problem to ponder: How could he suppress word of this massacre so that it would not reach any avenging American vessel? Kamehameha wisely decided the best course was to sever all shore-to-ship communication. It is most likely that he was privy to Metcalfe's letter demanding return of his boatswain. He instituted a *kapu,* and the *kapu* worked. If Metcalfe was bluffing, Kamehameha called it. In a few days he saw the *Eleanora* weigh anchor and head for the Orient. The king, who has been called merciless in battle, showed his favoritism by befriending two Europeans who would help him win a wide sovereignty.

10 ❦ Foiled

Plans for escape were on Young's and Davis's minds early on, despite the good treatment they received from Kamehameha. Young may or may not have wished to be reunited with the *Eleanora*, but it was a ship that provided a berth for a boatswain that many a seaman would have gladly accepted.

Young and Davis had been on the island for a year in early 1791, serving Kamehameha in warfare and in business dealings with traders and sailing vessels that dropped anchor off the coast of Hawai'i. One vessel that was offshore early in 1791 was that of Captain James Colnett, the *Argonaut*. By one means or another it came to his attention that two white men had been stranded and might well wish to find themselves on the high seas again.[1] Colnett took it upon himself to send a letter to the pair, stating that if they wished to repair to his ship he would provide all the protection and service possible. Colnett may have learned that one of these white men was John Young, the boatswain who perhaps had been bought over by Metcalfe in Canton two years prior. He would have been eager to assist Young and his colleague. Vancouver's account is that,

Young and Davis, being extremely averse to their present way of life concerted a plan for escaping to Captain Colnett's vessel, a measure very contrary to the wishes of Tamaahmaah lest revenge for the capture of the schooner [Fair American] *should follow their departure, to prevent which they were always very narrowly watched, and strongly guarded, whenever any vessel was in sight.*[2]

In his reply to Colnett, Young related the circumstances that had led to his current situation and accepted Colnett's offer to assist in his and Davis's escape. Unfortunately, a breakdown in communications soon occurred. The messenger whom Young employed to deliver the letter to Colnett met the high chief Kaiana and showed him the contents. This chief, already jealous of the two white men, took the letter to the king and persuaded him that he could read it, claiming that he had learned to read during a trip to China aboard an American vessel. Kaiana's version to

Kamehameha was that Young and Davis "desired Captain Colnett to get the king in his possession, and to keep him until the schooner and they were delivered up to him; and that he then should kill the king and many more of the islanders." To avoid this alleged trap, Kaiana urged the king to kill Young and Davis, "after which . . . no one would know any thing about them but themselves."

Colnett, sensing correctly that something had gone awry, sent a second letter, offering to help by sending anything to them that they needed, presumably to help in the escape. The messenger who took the letter returned with it the following day, having thought better of carrying out an act that could cost him his life. He had learned that Kamehameha had issued orders that any person attempting to carry anything from the two white men to Colnett, or in reverse, would be executed. According to Vancouver, who learned it from Young, "this disappointment determined them if possible to effect their escape." They would make their own plans to reach the ship.

Armed with their two muskets and some shot, they set out for the shore, but before reaching it they "were followed by a great number of inhabitants, who, being fearful of their guns, did not molest them." But what the natives lacked in arms they possessed in numbers. They prevented the two would-be escapees from moving out toward the ship, and in the melee Young, not wishing to fire his musket, swung it at one of the natives with a force that broke its stock. About this time Kamehameha arrived in a canoe with some of his attendants and instead of being angry,

very dispassionately advised them to return from whence they had come; and said, that he would do any thing they could wish to render their lives more comfortable, but that he could not consent that they should leave the island; assuring them that his people would rebel and put him to death, the instant they took their departure.

(This last sentence is considered "nonsense" by some historians. Either Young misspoke or Vancouver misunderstood.)

Kaiana, however, was not about to see such a happy ending, and he offered to take Young and Davis to Colnett's ship in his own canoe. But the king was not so easily deceived, and "well-knowing that Taiana [Kaiana] only wanted to accomplish their destruction, immediately interposed; and in the kindest and most persuasive manner requested that they would on no account accept Taiana's offer, but that they would return in his canoe with

J.Webber del

J.K.Sherwin sc.

Chapter 10

him." As Young later told Vancouver, Kamehameha assured him and Davis that there would be no "inconvenience suffered because of their attempt to escape, and the earnestness with which the king entreated them to return with him in his canoe, and let bygones be bygones, was readily accepted."

Vancouver learned from Young that "after this project was defeated neither he nor Davis were never suffered to be both afloat at the same time . . . and they were given to understand that the escape of one would be fatal to the other." Vancouver commented in his journal that this seemed to be a very political measure:

. . . as the interest they had in each other's happiness and welfare, and the sincere friendship and regard . . . between them, could not escape the observation of Tamaahmaah who would readily suggest the expediency of such an interdiction. Thus have Young and Davis since remained, observing that fidelity towards each other, which the true principles of honor dictate.

A high chief of Kona, Kaiana was among the first to greet and offer hospitality to Captain Cook. The latter was so impressed with Chief Kaiana that he commissioned his artist, John Webber, to execute a portrait of the chief. Kaiana had been to China and was considered well educated. He had no love for John Young and once plotted his death. At the outset of the Battle of Nuʻuanu he was a leader of a major detachment of Kamehameha's forces. The night before the initial attack Kaiana defected. He was killed in the battle a few days later.

11 ❧ To the Victor...

John Young found himself pressed into service of the warrior king almost immediately, as one of Kamehemeha's hopes was that the foreigners would teach him the ways of European warfare. Young, and probably Davis, was soon drilling the chief's warriors in the use of muskets and cannon. An army not unlike Western military modes was in the making.

Now that Kamehameha had two foreign gunners and the cannon Lopaka to assist him in battle, he lost no time moving onto Maui. It was in the spring of 1790,[1] only a month or two after both Young and Davis had been stranded on Hawai'i's shores. Davis had apparently recovered enough to assist in the invasion. The king's timing was right, for twice before his plans to take Maui had been dashed by Kahekili, chief of Maui and O'ahu. In the spring of 1790 Kahekili was on O'ahu, and the Hawai'i Island forces landed at Kahului beach and moved inland, forcing the Maui defenders into the cul-de-sac of Iao Valley. It was a fatal move for the men of Maui, for Young and Davis maneuvered the cannon Lopaka from Kahului to the opening of the valley, and there aimed directly into the throat of Iao Valley.

Kahekili's son, Kalanikūpule, was routed, and he escaped over the mountains, later joining his father on O'ahu. Meanwhile Young and Davis, along with Kamehameha's trained warriors, had taken a heavy toll on the besieged defenders. It had been a slaughter. The bodies of the dead clogged the mountain stream. Scores of fighting men had fallen before the cannon and swivel guns that would go on to win Kamehameha even more battles. The Iao battle came to be called "Kepaniwai," meaning the damming of the waters, after the bodies of fallen Maui soldiers that clogged the stream.

There was no lull for the king to bask in the glory of his victory. Trouble had broken out on his home island of Hawai'i, and Kamehameha's visit to Moloka'i, for reconciliation with chiefess Kalola, was cut short. Before leaving he sent to Kahekili, on O'ahu, two small stones, one white, one black, offering peace or war. Kahekili's response was for Kamehameha to wait until he was dead before coming to O'ahu.[2]

For now it was on to more war on Hawai'i's windward coast, to repel the chief Keōua, who had advanced into Hamakua and Kohala. In his

Young and Davis training Hawaiians in the use of the small cannon, named Lopaka. When on deck the weapon would have been maneuvered on small wheels. Even if the Hawaiians had had wheels they would have had difficulty hauling the cannon over rough terrain. Modification allowed the whole assembly be a sort of sled that could be lashed in place and pulled by ropes in front or behind. The cannon, which played a large part in the battles of Nuʻuanu and Iao Valley, could be removed from the carriage and carried separately, slung from long poles resting on many strong shoulders. Illustration by Herb Kawainui Kāne. Collection of the author

march to Waimea, Keōua had used the "scorched earth" method of demoralizing the population. Taro fields were uprooted, fish ponds opened and destroyed, villages burnt, and coconut trees felled. Kamehameha, accompanied by Young, pursued the enemy back down the coast, almost to Hilo. There the two forces engaged in a bitter and futile battle. Both sides withdrew to lick their wounds. The only victor, wrote Kuykendall, was death.[3]

Some weeks later John Young was at Kawaihae. It was November of 1790 when he reportedly saw in the distance a high plume of ash, smoke, and steam shooting upward from the other side of Mauna Loa. It was Kilauea belching from distant Halemaʻumaʻu crater, a sight that had perhaps seldom been seen from that part of the island. The eruption of 1790 is considered among the most awesome and terrifying to occur in the Hawaiian chain in historic times. The site of this massive explosion was about sixty miles from Young's north Hawaiʻi Island location. By calculating the horizontal distance between Young's point of observation and Kilauea crater, which lay on the eastern slope of Mokuweoweo, it is estimated that the smoke and ash were shooting at least twenty-five thousand feet high, about four to five miles.[4]

What was a spectacular attraction for Young and other spectators was a disaster for Keōua, who was moving his troops south from Hilo to Ka'ū:

The path they followed ran by the crater. . . . While they were camped at that place the volcano burst forth in a terrific explosive eruption, sending up dense clouds of smoke intermixed with stones, ashes and suffocating gases. This was repeated at intervals for several days. Apparently Keōua and his warriors were safe in their camp, but they were filled with terror and anxious to get away. On the third day they started out in three divisions, but had not gone far when the most terrific eruption of the whole series took place.[5]

Keōua's center division was caught in this freak and devastating eruption. That part of the army, along with the many women and children who accompanied it, were killed outright. It is estimated that about four hundred died, mostly by asphyxiation. It would have been unusual for many to be killed by falling rocks. Evidence of the plight of Keōua's fleeing foot soldiers is seen today in footprints solidified in ash on the surface of the lava fields in the Ka'ū desert, about seven miles from Kilauea's Halema'uma'u crater.

Many were convinced that Pele, the famed, feared, and revered goddess of fire and Hawai'i's volcanoes, was displeased with Keōua and showed it by causing the eruption. But this powerful young Hawai'i Island chief was not deterred by what most considered Pele's wrath. Kamehameha, on the other hand, ever devout in his worship of Pele, saw this as a sign of Pele's support.

Earlier, Kamehameha had pondered over how he might win the favor of the war god Kūkā'ilimoku and thus become sole ruler of all Hawai'i Island. He sought the wisdom of a Kaua'i *kahuna* (priest), who told the king's messenger that he must construct a great new temple, or *heiau*, to the war god. It was to be located at Pu'ukoholā, a sizable lofty mound just outside of Kawaihae, where it would face the sea and remain forever as tribute to the war god. If this were done, Kamehameha was told, he could "gain the kingdom without a scratch to his skin."[6]

Thus Kamehameha set out to accomplish a task that would ultimately take more than a year and the labor of thousands of men from all the island's districts. The specific site for the *heiau* was chosen by *kahuna* who were meticulous in determining, with the help of their gods, site design, measurements, and layout. Work parties from all over the island labored in relays as thousands upon thousands of stones, some boulder size, were carried up to the site for the main temple and platforms. The logistics of simply providing food and shelter for this vast number of workers are staggering. Commoners and chiefs of all ranks worked side by side carrying and placing stones. Even Kamehameha put his shoulders to the task and labored to complete the huge project. There is no evidence that John Young participated, for it may well have been a task reserved only for devotees of the war god, Kūkā'ilimoku. But he did observe what went on and later commented that he had seen at least thirteen humans sacrificed there.[7]

Another outbreak of war interrupted the completion of the *heiau* for many months. Kahekili and Ka'eo retook the islands of Moloka'i and Maui. Kamehameha knew he had to deal with these reverses and was determined for a fight to the finish. This was probably in the spring of 1791.[8] It began and ended in a naval battle, quite likely the greatest in Hawai'i's history. One factor in making it a sea battle unlike any other was the involvement of the armed *Fair American*. The two challenging chieftains crossed from Maui to the upper northeast coast of Hawai'i Island in a fleet of canoes filled with warriors armed with spears and javelins. They also carried firearms and a cannon, which came from visiting foreign vessels willing to trade and sell weapons for provisions. Such formidable weapons denied Kamehameha the advantage of being the only fighter with modern European weapons, such as his Lopaka and swivel guns on the *Fair American*.

Kamehameha met the invaders head-on with his well-armed fleet of double canoes. While Kahekili had some Europeans to man his cannons, John Young and Isaac Davis manned the swivels and cannon on Kamehameha's schooner. These two veterans of the sea proved expert artillerymen, and to them the perceived success of the battle off Waimanu Valley may be attributed. Because of the fire force employed by both sides, the battle became known, and is still recorded as, *Kekūwaha'ulaula,* "Battle of the Red-Mouthed Gun." It was not a decisive battle, despite the fact that Kahekili and Ka'eo withdrew to Maui. History has judged Kamehameha the victor. Both Ka'eo and Kahekili returned to Maui "and began immediately to prepare for the return invasion, which they had every reason to expect from Kamehameha."[9]

Kamehameha aboard the Fair American *converses with his advisors Young and Davis as his war fleet approaches Maui.*
©*Herb Kawainui Kāne.*
Collection of the artist

The Battle of the Red-Mouthed Gun, off Waimanu Valley, spring 1790.

Painting by Herb Kawainui Kāne. Army Museum, Fort DeRussy, Honolulu.

© *National Geographic Society, Washington, D.C.*

H. Kawainui Kane

With the business of battle behind him for the time being, Kamehameha turned his efforts and energy, and that of his vast array of workers, to the completion of Puʻukoholā, the second largest *heiau* ever built in Hawaiʻi and certainly one of the largest in all of Polynesia. It was probably completed in mid-1791.

Kamehameha, having completed the *heiau*, felt that it was time to talk of peace on the island of which he was only part ruler. Two of his long-faithful chiefs, Keaweheulu and Kamanawa, were chosen as bearers of an invitation to Keōua from Kamehameha to meet vis-à-vis and talk of laying down arms and raising up peace. The site for the ceremony would be at Kawaihae, in the shadow of the immense temple to Kūkāʻilimoku.

Keōua agreed to accompany the two emissaries back to Kawaihae, accompanied by members of his court and trusted warriors—a total of twenty-seven canoes. Did he believe the Kilauea catastrophe was a sign of Pele's support for Kamehameha? Did he have a premonition of death? Kuykendall wrote:

Just before arriving at that place he [Keōua] arranged his company so that he had with him in his own double canoe chiefs who would be proper death companions for him, while the others were ordered to go in another canoe with his younger brother Kaoleioku. Thus they entered the bay; on a hill overlooking it was the great heiau; near the shore, with his retinue about him, was Kamehameha, resplendent in feather cloak and helmet.[10]

Keōua was likewise outfitted in regalia intended for a great ceremony. Kamakau surmises, like Kuykendall, that Keōua foresaw his end:

He brought out all his weapons of war, his feather capes and feather helmets, and placed them in . . . canoes. He also ranged his own chiefs about him in his double canoe, those of high rank and those who had lived with him, and upon whose love he could count and who would die with him. Such was the custom with chiefs of old to have many companions in death. Keōua knew that he was about to die, and those who were with him.[11]

Some of Keōua's followers traveled over the mountains to be with their leader at the designated meeting place. The chief and his retinue sailed in their many canoes up the Kona side of the island. They passed Puakō, then approached Kawaihae Bay, where Kamehameha and his considerable royal entourage stood on the shore. John Young would have been among them.

At some distance from each other the two kings exchanged greetings and then Keōua prepared to disembark from his canoe. But at that moment Ke'eaumoku, who was nearby with a group of retainers, hurled his spear at Keōua and, after a brief struggle, killed him. Keōua's immediate companions, those who were with him in his canoe, were likewise killed by Ke'eaumoku and his followers, [some by musket fire from the shore]. Then Kamehameha intervened to stop the slaughter and save the lives of Kaoleioku and those who were with him.[12]

The fallen chief's body was carried to the great Pu'ukoholā Heiau, where it was offered, as others would be, at the altar as a sacrifice. Kamakau wrote:

When Kaihekioi saw the chief Keoua being born on men's shoulders to Puukohola he chanted these words of affectionate lament. "My lord of the rain of Ha'ao, The rain flies fast, Flies over the upland of 'Au'aulele, The rain flies driven by the wind. The rain drives down from the cliffs above, The tears for my chief Drop down on the heads of the people."[13]

Ha'ao is the name of a rain that comes down at Waiohinu in Ka'ū and keeps that district green. It is also the name of the spring second in size of the five springs that water Waiohinu. The chant was still being chanted in 1934 by the old people of Ka'ū district, many of whom retained their love of Keōua and their disdain of Kamehameha.

Historians remain divided as to whether or not the slaying was pre-arranged. Did Kamehameha sanction such a treachery, or was it the fault of the spear-happy and impetuous Ke'eaumoku? There are those who saw it as a flagrant act of violence by a king who wanted his main adversary removed. Kamehameha did indeed acquire the lands and sphere of influence that were once Keōua's. He was now the master of all the island of Hawai'i. Kamehameha would let peace reign, at least for the next three years. He knew that to weld all the islands into one, he must first conquer O'ahu and then bring into his realm the northern island of Kaua'i.

Peace reigned for the next three years, but then plans for an attack on O'ahu soon unfurled. Kamehameha was prepared to attack, but timing was of upmost importance. In January 1795 two English trading ships, the *Jackall* and the *Lee Boo,* were in Honolulu Harbor. The king of O'ahu, Kalanikūpule, and his chiefs attempted to commandeer the ships, which were carrying much ammunition and arms. They were thwarted in their attempt, but not before killing the captains of both ships. The ships' mates,

A ceremony at Puʻukoholā Heiau, one of the largest temples in all of Polynesia. Snow-clad Mauna Kea rises in the background. © *Herb Kawainui Kāne. Collection of the National Park Service*

The arrival of rival chief Keōua at Kawaihae. Puʻukoholā Heiau surmounts the hill in the background. © Herb Kawainui Kāne. Collection of the National Park Service

Lamport and Bonallack, were now in command, and they made a speedy departure for Canton. Before leaving they left with Young and Davis, presumably at Kawaihae, a letter informing them of Kalanikūpule's plan to attack Hawai'i, advising them to warn Kamehameha.

Kamehameha decided to strike at once and moved fast to do so. In the past three years he had prepared by building hundreds of canoes to supplement those that his chiefs and lesser warriors would provide for an invasion of O'ahu. The canoe-building task was arduous and time consuming. Much of it took place in Hilo, an area dear to Kamehameha and where there was an abundance of large trees. Three years was barely enough time, for hundreds of koa trees had to be felled, hauled from the forests to the beaches, then hollowed out and shaped into sleek, swift canoes, each capable of carrying as many as fifty warriors. By midsummer of 1795 the armada was ready to attack, but there was unfinished business for the king. En route to O'ahu he would retake Lāna'i and Maui, territory he had once won then lost to the now deceased Kahekili. This time the defenders were easily overcome, and Moloka'i offered no resistance.

It was on the west end of Moloka'i that the king's forces, thousands of them, encamped before launching the predawn attack. Charles Bishop, commander of the ship *Ruby,* reported:

In addition to their other Forces they had the schooner . . . loaded with the train of artillery consisting of twelve guns, from 3 to 6 pounders, Powder, Shott, and Military Stores. This part was under the direction of John Young, assisted by six other English besides which there was one or more English in the vanguard of each division.[14]

During the night Kamehameha held a strategy session including his advisors, Young and Davis, and all his chiefs. That is, all except Kaiana, "the turbulent chief." A noble and able chieftain in his own right, Kaiana was ambitious for the power that now lay in Kamehameha's hands. The king knew the jealous nature of this handsome high chief, and he knew that Young and Davis were objects of Kaiana's distrust. Although he had reservations about Kaiana's loyalty, he nonetheless gave him a division to lead into battle. This, Kaiana reasoned, was the ripe time to strike out on his own, join Kalanikūpule's forces, defeat Kamehameha, and make himself king of Hawai'i Island. Once in the channel off Moloka'i he swung his division to the right, toward O'ahu's windward coast. There he joined the

Chapter 11

O'ahu forces that would come up over the steep Nu'uanu *pali* and attack Kamehameha head on, but he soon discovered that his efforts were in vain.

Kamehameha's fleet and forces met meager resistance as they landed on the southeast shores of O'ahu; in fact, they had an opportunity to rest before moving inland. The invading troops were stretched all the way from the beach at Waialae, westward past Lē'ahi (Diamond Head), past Waikiki, and as far west as the village known as Kou (present site of Honolulu Harbor), where the *Fair American* and the *Britannia* dropped anchor. The opposition they met ended up in skirmishes with minimal loss of life on both sides. A minor battle took place off Puowaina crater (Punchbowl). From that point on the invaders pressed the defenders back farther and farther into Nu'uanu Valley.

The principal battle was fought in the fairly flat lands of Pū'iwa and Laimi, the site of today's O'ahu Country Club. It was at Pū'iwa that the warrior chieftain, the renegade Kaiana, was felled by a spear. Here may have been fought the fiercest battle—hand to hand combat, deadly daggers, war clubs, javelins, and spears all drew copious amounts of Hawaiian blood. Kamehameha's soldiers, who had been drilled by Vancouver and now directed by Young and Davis, performed as semiprofessionals. The frequent flashes of many muskets from both sides took their toll, but the defenders offered no offense against the artillery aimed into their midst by Young and Davis. It was the Battle of the Red-Mouthed Gun all over again, only on land. The O'ahuans were pressed deeper and deeper into Nu'uanu Valley, whose wooded walls offered slight escape. The only other breakout, at the valley's end, was a sheer drop of a thousand feet. That was the fate of literally hundreds of Kalanikūpule's troops, who were forced to the valley's abrupt edge. Some were able to escape by climbing the ridges on either side. The O'ahu king made his escape into the high, cold and damp mountains, only to be captured months later in central O'ahu and put to death. But the vast majority were pushed to the edge of the cliff, where they plunged to their death upon the rocks below.

The entire battle was fought and won by Kamehameha in about a week's time. It would be his last major battle and the most decisive. He was

OVERLEAF:

Young and Davis were among Kamehameha's lieutenants in the 1795 campaign on O'ahu, which ended at Nu'uanu Pali when the O'ahu army, unable to escape, was driven over the edge of the pali *(cliff). Painting by Herb Kawainui Kāne. Kamehameha Schools/Bishop Estate*

not yet forty-three years old by the time he was to conquer all the islands save Kaua'i. A contemporary account of the invasion of O'ahu was reported in 1796 by Charles Bishop:[15]

Soon after the deaths of the English Captains at Woahoo, and the recapture of their vessels by their crews, Tom Himay Haw the King of Owhyee, having had intelligence of the proceeding and Intentions of the people of Woahoo, and also of the vessels being retaken. By the desire of all of his chiefs, and advice of his White Friends, prepared a most formidable army of at least 10,000 warriors, with a fleet divided into four divisions, each consisting of three hundred canoes, for the purpose of subjecting Woahoo, and the intermediate Isles, Mowee, Rani, and Morotai.

And as the English say, to avenge the deaths of Captain Brown and his officers.

This formidable fleet set sail from Owhyhee last June. . . . In addition to their other Force they had the schooner, who was loaded with the train of artillery, consisting of twelve guns, from 3 to 6 pounders, Powder, Shott, and Military Stores, this part of the Force was under the Direction of John Young, assisted by six other English, besides which, there was one or more English in the vanguard of each division, who are esteemed good warriors, (even by the Sandwich Islanders), they met with little or no opposition in conquering the Isles of Mowee and Morotai, and having thus subjected them . . . the army proceeded toward Woahoo, and arriving there about the middle of August, they landed in three different parts of the Island meeting at First with little opposition. Tianna . . . was a principal chief in one of these divisions; who having conceived some cause or affront from the King, went over to the Enemy.

The Battle of Nu'uanu is of such significance that it is still being commemorated two centuries later.[16]

    The conquering king lost no time in making plans for an assault on the island of Kaua'i, to complete his sovereignty over the Hawaiian chain. But before he could reorganize his troops and reassemble a fleet to overcome King Kaumualii, trouble in the form of a rebellion broke out on the home front. It was in the Hilo area and was fomented by a disgruntled brother of Kaiana named Namakeha. Kamehameha's forces put down the uprising in a matter of months.

    By the middle of 1796 the king was poised to launch the attack on Kaua'i and its island satellite, Ni'ihau. After appropriate offerings to the gods, the fleet sailed northwest from Oʻahu into the wide and rough channel that separates the two islands. But the gods apparently were not appeased, for soon several canoes were overturned and others swamped by a strong storm that sprang up in the channel. The only course was to turn back and once again, at a later date, appeal to the gods. It would be six more years, until 1802, before Kamehameha was able to give serious attention to another attempted invasion of the island of Kauaʻi. From 1796 until 1802 this "Garibaldi of Hawaii" was again entering into trade arrangements with foreigners, as usual negotiated by John Young, who was still regarded as the king's chief advisor in such matters. The king, back on his home island again, used the next two years to rebuild an armada of at least two schooners and eight hundred war canoes capable of carrying thousands of armed warriors and much modern European weaponry—muskets and cannon.

Late in 1802, after a long layover at Lahaina, Kamehameha's fleet was set to be launched from Oʻahu for the invasion of Kauaʻi. By Young's account, over seven thousand native warriors and fifty *haole*s, most with muskets, comprised the fighting strength. An abundance of ammunition, forty swivel guns, and six mortars were aboard the schooners and war canoes. King Kaumualii was vastly outnumbered in both warriors and weapons.

But in mid-1803 disaster struck again, with great finality. This time it was in the form of a devastating epidemic, perhaps cholera (some say it was the black death). With no immunity to the white man's diseases, natives were felled by the hundreds, then by the thousands, on all islands. Carried away by sudden death were high chiefs, great leaders, and trained warriors, the very men vital to the success of the invasion. Even Kamehameha was stricken but recovered. He was now convinced that his gods did not approve of his goals, despite the human sacrifices that he had offered them. The Oʻahu decimation of his warriors rendered an invasion impossible. It was called off, never to be attempted again.

By 1810 Kamehameha was willing to heed advice that would bring about a negotiated peace. This was successfully accomplished by an American sea captain, Nathan Winship, and it left Kaumualii as king of Kauaʻi, but under the rule of Kamehameha, a situation that neither relished.

John Young had not been an active player in the Kauaʻi invasion plans. According to John Boit, Young wished that the king would give up the idea of attacking Kauaʻi, "for there was a considerable number of Bottany [*sic*] Bay gentry there who would fight desperately."[17] It was just prior to the 1802 planned attack on Kauaʻi that Kamehameha appointed Young governor of Hawaiʻi Island, a post he held for a decade. Neither Young nor his colleague Davis had to wait for a Kauaʻi conquest to become recipients of Kamehameha's appreciation for their input and action. Rewards of generous land grants were swift and significant.

Although Young was not an active player in the planned Kauaʻi invasion, or its negotiated acquisition by Kamehameha, Isaac Davis was perhaps too much so. Davis and his family were already living on Oʻahu well before the 1810 settlement. He was very much involved with traders and in doing business on Oʻahu for the king, and he also had his ear to the ground. Just prior to Kaumualii's scheduled visit to Oʻahu, Davis learned that some of the chiefs, disgruntled at the thought of the Kauaʻi king getting what they thought was too good a deal, contrived to poison Kaumualii. He transmitted this information to the Kauaʻi chiefs, and the plot failed. Angry at having been thwarted by Davis's intervention, the Oʻahu schemers turned the tables. It has never been definitely proven that Davis, who died in April 1810, was poisoned, but circumstances strongly indicate that the Welsh sailor and friend of Kamehameha died a wrongful death at the hands of those whose plans he had thwarted.

12 ❦ The Vancouver Visits

Thirteen years had passed since George Vancouver had last been in the Sandwich Islands. He first visited them as a midshipman in the service of Captain James Cook, and from the deck of his vessel he had seen the young Kamehameha, whom he later recalled as having looked ferocious. Now, in 1791, he had, like Cook, earned a captaincy. The honor had been conferred upon the thirty-one-year-old naval officer by the British Admiralty in 1785, in recognition of his demonstrated ability and the Admiralty's conviction that he would bring honor and prestige to his country. He did indeed, and came to be regarded as a great navigator in the tradition of Cook himself. In 1789 the Admiralty gave Vancouver the considerable task of exploring the Northwest Coast of the North American continent, an unfinished task of Captain Cook's. He was to winter in the Sandwich Islands and also to survey them.[1] He was also given a much more sensitive diplomatic assignment—to resolve the Nootka dispute, which involved the return of British lands from Spanish authorities who had earlier taken possession.

Vancouver made three visits to the islands on this expedition. The first, which lasted three weeks, took place in March and April of 1792, and it was the shortest of his visits. There is no indication that he met with either Kamehameha or John Young during this visit. On Kauaʻi he met the young chief Kaumualii, who later became king of that island.[2]

Vancouver returned to the islands a year later, in February and March 1793. During this visit he not only met Kamehameha and other notable chieftains, but also a countryman, John Young. This second visit "was the first time since the night off Maui in November, 1778, that Kamehameha and Vancouver had met and the surprise was mutual and a sincere friendship sprang up between the two."[3] Young's presence was important not only because of his British origins, but also for his value as an interpreter. Vancouver wrote: "Tamaahmaah [Kamehameha] came on board in a very large canoe, accompanied by John Young, an English seaman, who appeared to be not only a great favourite but to possess no small degree of influence with this great chief."[4]

*The English explorer and navigator Captain George Vancouver
held Kamehameha, Young, and Davis in high esteem.*

Painting by Philip Hale after the original by Lemuel Abbott.

Bishop Museum, Honolulu

Vancouver's impressions of the Hawaiian king and his followers were not only favorable but laudatory. In his account from "His Britannic Majesty's Ship Discovery, March 8, 1793 Kealakekua Bay, Hawai'i," Vancouver wrote:

I beg leave to inform all Commanders of Vessels and into whose hands this testimony may fall, that on February 21, 1793, I was visited at sea by Tamaahmaah the sole acknowledged King of Hawai'i . . . with the people under his authority supplied us with water, wood and all kinds of refreshments in the greatest profusion, for which they received neither arms nor ammunition, but cheerfully and eagerly disposed of these commodities for other articles of commerce infinitely more useful and necessary to their comfort. And I have the greatest pleasure in informing those whom it may concern, that Tamaahmaah, with the generality of the Chiefs, and the . . . people have conducted themselves towards us with the strictest honesty, civility, and friendly attention.

Vancouver then identified the various chiefs who had visited. He added, "But I fear Tiaanna [Kaiana], and his brother Namakeha are not much to be trusted."

Of Kamehameha's favorite wife, Ka'ahumanu, Vancouver observed that she appeared "to be about sixteen, and undoubtedly did credit to the choice and taste of Tamaahmaah being one of the finest women we have yet seen on any of the islands. It was pleasing to observe the kindness and fond attention, with which on all occasions they seemed to regard each other."

Earlier, Vancouver had recorded that he had met three seamen, John Young, Isaac Davis, and John Smith, whom he believed to be subjects of Great Britain:

At least they [Young and Davis], have acknowledged themselves under my authority, and for advice and diverse essential reasons I have given them my permission still to remain on this Island: I therefore, in the name of the King, my master, recommend them to be treated with civility, kindness and hospitality, not only by the subjects of Great Britain but also of all other powers or states who may meet with them.

Vancouver characterized Kamehameha as being benevolent,

humane, and of a friendly nature. Also, on his third and last visit in 1794 he found the king's conduct to have been of such "a most princely nature . . . and for his friendly and good behavior I caused a large boat to be built and given him, called the Britannia, her size, and beam mentioned in a plate of copper, nailed to the stern of the vessel." One might well wager that there were few island kings anywhere who were recipients of such a practical and valuable gift. The ship was built under the direction of an Englishman named James Boyd, a skilled shipwright. With help from Vancouver's carpenters, the able assistance of Isaac Davis, and twenty canoe makers apprenticed by Kamehameha under the guidance of John Young, a fine seaworthy vessel was produced. It had a keel of twenty-nine feet and a beam of more than nine.[5] It was to be Kamehameha's first man o' war, and it would serve the king well. It pleased Vancouver to see Kamehameha, "who, for the purpose of obtaining such knowledge as might hereafter enable him to follow the example of our artificers, had paid the strictest attention to all their proceedings in the construction of the Britannia." It was also typical of the king, who had an innate curiosity and was eager to learn about new things.

A good judge of men, Vancouver was appreciative of the observations that Young and Davis made of the local chiefs and "the leading people on the island. I derived from them such information respecting the conduct of certain chiefs, as may be considered important: at least to those whose pursuits may lead them to these seas."

In his journal Vancouver noted that instead of seeing the savage countenance he had once observed in Kamehameha, "I was agreeably surprised in finding that his riper years had softened that stern ferocity which his younger days had exhibited . . . and he had changed his general deportment to an address characteristic of an open, cheerful and sensible mind; combined with great generosity and goodness of disposition."

As for others that came aboard Vancouver's vessel from the island,

I was very much pleased with the decorum and general conduct of the royal party [who were] particularly cautious to avoid giving the least cause for offense. . . . We first learned from Young that our royal visitors did not entertain the most distant idea of accepting any thing until they had first set the example.

Among the gifts that Vancouver did leave were cattle and sheep. But the hogs he received as gifts were far in excess of the needs for the crew.

It was from John Young that Vancouver learned firsthand of the disaster at Olowalu, and it was Vancouver's account that went into history books. As for the schooner *Fair American*, Kamehameha assured the navigator that it was his intention to return it to Captain Metcalfe and set things right. "Young bore witness to the king's sincerity . . . but from Young we learned that the schooner was of little value, having nearly fallen to pieces for want of necessary repairs," Vancouver wrote.

Early on Vancouver expressed his conviction that neither Young nor Davis were deserters. Nor were they on the island by their own choice, "but from a series of events impossible to foresee or provide against." He noted that their behavior on the island had been

meritorious in the highest sense of the word; support[ed] by their character (for they possessed nothing else) . . . that it insured them of the respect . . . affections and regard, of the natives; and of no one more than of the king himself, who did not fail to listen to their counsel and advice.

It was Young and Davis to whom Vancouver said he was "indebted for the friendly and hospitable reception . . . and for the civil behaviour . . . from the natives, by their attention to the instructions and examples of these our countrymen." He encouraged them "at all times to be useful and assisting to the subjects of every civilized power, who might resort to Owhyhee." From the king and his immediate chiefs Vancouver received a promise for the continuance of the couple's protection, "not only to their persons, but to their property also; particularly a large assortment of useful and necessary articles that I had given them."

Kamehameha told Vancouver his plans to bring all the islands under his control, and explained that it could happen only by subduing the occupants of those islands. This Vancouver deplored, for he was not unaware of the suffering of the inhabitants and the large loss of life in such battles as had already involved the king. He endeavored to persuade Kamehameha that negotiations with the rulers of the other islands would be a much more practical and peaceful way of achieving his goal. The king listened and heard Vancouver out, but he was not persuaded. He knew only one way of winning, and it was by warfare.

At one point Vancouver became involved in a dispute between a Hawai'i Island chief and a Maui ruler. In an endeavor to bring about a successful, and peaceful, conclusion, it was agreed, wrote Vancouver,

that I should upon my arrival on Mowee use my endeavors to establish a
permanent peace on my own principles: and, by a letter to Young from
thence, inform Tamaahmaah with the progress of my negotiacion, which
they promised to do and ratify, if a chief, properly authorized, brought the
letter from Mowee.

Young's role in further negotiations is not clarified in the captain's journal.

During his two last visits, Vancouver had ample opportunity to observe the important roles played by Young and Davis. In addition to making frequent references to them, he specifically cited their value to Kamehameha. He noted that they resided "intirely with Tamaahmaah, are in his most perfect confidence, attend him in all his executions of business or pleasure, or expeditions of war or enterprize; and are in the habit of daily experiencing from him the greatest respect, and the highest degree of esteem and regard."

He mentioned not only the lands given the two able advisors by Kamehameha, but also that "the next chiefs in power" have shown them great respect and friendship. Vancouver himself was obviously much impressed by these two natives from his own land, whom he referred to as "our two countrymen." It was typical of Vancouver to be so taken with Young and Davis that he offered "these two worthy characters" free passage to their homeland.

After much consideration they preferred their present way of life . . .
observing that being destitute of resources on their return home (which,
however, they spoke of in a way that did honor to their hearts and under-
standings), they might again be exposed to the vicissitudes of a life of hard
labour, for the purpose of merely acquiring a precarious supply of the most
common necessaries of life; objects for which for some years past, had not
occasioned them the least concern. . . . Here they lived happily, and in the
greatest plenty; and, to their praise be it spoken, the principal object . . . was
to correct by gentle means the vices, and encourage by the most laudable
endeavours the virtues of these islanders.

Vancouver opined that "there are reasonable grounds to believe, that, by steadily pursuing their same line of conduct, it will in time have a due influence on the general character of these people."[6]

It was a thoughtful George Vancouver who, upon his return to England, notified the newspapers of his encounter with Young and Davis. A grateful sister, Sarah Davis, saw the notice and wrote to a long lost brother:

London, May 2, 1799

Mr. Isaac Davis At Owhyhee Sandwich Islands

Dear Brother: With a heart overwhelmed with joy mixt with sorrow do I sit down to write to you and I make no doubt but you will be surprised to receive the Same. The first time that I had any Account of You was Advertised in the Newspapers which was as follows

> *Isaac Davis of Milfordhaven and John Young of Liverpool is on the Island of Owhyhee this was the Intelligence that Captain Vancouver gave upon his Return which allarm'd us beyond Expression to think that you was Confined in an Unknown Land who we thought Dead and Lost to us forever in this Life and has Caused us many heartfelt Moment and in particular your Dear and Aged Mother who has from the first Moment you Left home been in Continual Sorrow for her Dear Son whom she thought had shared the same death as your father and Brother did. Our Dear Mother is still Living and as Well as Can be Expected of Old Age. She gives her Blessing to You and that the Almighty God May Protect and Watch over you and that he may once more Restore his Lost Child to her and his Native Country which would be of more Value to her than all the Riches of the Indias Thank God we are all Living and Settled in Credit and our Dear Mother wants for Nothing She Still lives in the same place We beg that you will write at all Opportunitys as you know where we are if we don't know how to Direct to You There is no fear but Some of us will receive them as we are so well known I hope You will Receive this Safe all Your Sisters Join in Love to you and all begs that you will endeavour to Come the first Opportunity You Can get as we Shall all be Anxious for Your Return We all Join in Love to Mr. Young Your fellow traveller and faithful Companion Whom we Respect and Regard on Your Account as You Must be More than Brothers My Ever Dear Brother I have the happiness to inform You that I have Seen a Gentleman that told me he saw you in perfect health Eighteen Months Ago he Belong to a Vessell that went out on Discoveries his Wife was on Board with him which Gentlewoman you saw and Conversed with at times the Gentleman's name is [. . .] who has been so kind as to forward this to You You will direct Your Letter Mrs. Davis Hubberstonferry Milfordhaven South Wales My Dear Brother I Conclude with my kind Love and Sincerest Wishes for Your Welfare and Speedy return from your Affectionate Sister til Death. Sarah Davis*

There is no indication that any of the Young family saw Vancouver's notice that Young and Davis were alive and in Hawai'i.

Lieutenant Peter Puget, like Vancouver, also commented upon the desire of the two men to remain in the islands, although "Davis wished once more to see England, but after that would be glad to reside here the rest of his days." In Puget's remarks of January 13, 1794, he wrote:

Both were perfectly satisfied with their Situation, especially Young, who said that habituated to a life of Ease and Tranquility, he did not like to launch once more into the Busy World where he was certain that the only Sustenance he could expect must be by hard labour. In this Island he was treated with Respect by all Ranks and had all the necessaries of life, nay, even the Luxuries given him.[7]

Prior to his departure, Vancouver delivered to Young and Davis "such testimonials of their good conduct as I considered them intitled to, for the purpose of securing to them the respect and confidence of future visitors, who would be warned by them of the snares and dangers they were liable to."

Three weeks before leaving "Owhyhee" Island for further nautical and astronomical observations on the other islands, Kamehameha and Vancouver entered into various transactions in "this hospitable port," Kealakekua. Whatever the transactions were, perhaps trading and encampments, none measured up to one, which might well have made Great Britain the ultimate ruler of the Sandwich Islands. Kamehameha was already well disposed toward Great Britain by virtue of his two trustworthy advisors, Young and Davis, and now the genuine friendship and admiration of Captain Vancouver. Cession to "His Brittanic Majesty became now an object of his serious concern."

It is most conceivable that Kamehameha's decision was not made without input from Young and Davis. Not only were they natives of the nation he admired, but Kamehameha had found their advice helpful in other matters of state, as well as of war. Perhaps they persuaded him of the value of being a protectorate of the English crown rather than of another world power such as France, Russia, or even the fledgling United States of America. Kamehameha and Vancouver had discussed the subject the year prior, and Kamehameha now came to view the union as one that would offer protection from other powers. In the intervening months, and before

Vancouver's third and final visit of 1794, the matter was discussed at a council of the chiefs, where the pros and cons were weighed and deliberated. The chiefs agreed to their king's proposal. In their 1794 mid-February meeting, Kamehameha assured Vancouver that he was now in a position to cede his island kingdom to George III of England, and in turn he was assured that Vancouver would carry that message to his monarch half a world away.

Once accord was reached, a grand ceremony was held on the shore, where the British flag was raised and the vessels fired their salutes. "Vancouver took possession of Hawai'i [Island, not the chain] for His Brittanic Majesty."[8] About the same time, a copper plate was affixed to the king's residence, which read:

On the 25th of February, 1794, Tamaahmaah, king of Owhyhee, in council with the principal chiefs of the island, assembled on board his Brittanic Majesty's sloop Discovery, in Karakakooa bay, in the presence of George Vancouver, commander of the said sloop; Lieutenant Peter Puget, commander of his said Majesty's tender the Chatham; and the other officers of the Discovery; after due consideration, unanimously ceded the said island of Owhyhee to his Brittanic Majesty, and acknowledged themselves to be subjects of Great Britain.[9]

According to Kuykendall and other historians, nothing ever came of this event. The British government took no action, and "its legal force must since have long lapsed."[10] Nonetheless, the word spread that Hawai'i was a protectorate of Great Britain, and this afforded Kamehameha a defense he could not have purchased. Only Vancouver's failure to present the document for formal cession, or parliament's failure to act upon it, kept Hawai'i from becoming part of the British empire "beyond the seas." Significantly, patterns of the Union Jack appear in Hawai'i's flag.

The departure of the *Discovery* on the morning of March 3, 1794, was tinged with sadness for both the Hawaiians and Vancouver. Kamehameha expressed the wish that the great captain would soon return, and said he would long remember his kindness. Vancouver, for his part, expressed gratitude for past favors and even then the great amount of refreshments which the natives bestowed upon him and the crew. One gift that Vancouver would not give, to those chiefs who asked for them, and white men who also desired them, were muskets and ammunition. He was firm in his determination not to contribute to warfare or violence brought about by such means. He felt strongly that "putting firearms into the hands of uncivilized people is, at best very bad policy; but when they are given in an imperfect and insufficient condition for a valuable consideration, it is not only infamously fraudulent, but barbarous and inhuman." He deplored and condemned those trading ships that put arms and ammunition in the hands of the natives.

The captain did not overlook leaving for Young and Davis "such an assortment of useful articles for promoting their comforts, as it was within our power to afford." It is quite likely that the Bible that Young would later treasure and read was a Vancouver gift. After the departure Vancouver wrote in his journal, "Our two countrymen, Young and Davis, bid us farewell with a degree of reluctance that did credit to their feelings."

Kuykendall says that Vancouver's relations with Young and Davis had historical significance:

He repeatedly speaks in high praise of those humble British seamen who in a short space of time had become Hawaiian chiefs. He approved of their decision to stay rather than to return to England. . . . He believed they could be of essential service in strengthening the alliance between Hawai`i and Great Britain.[11]

Kuykendall recognized that it is difficult to tell which of the three Englishmen—Vancouver, Young, or Davis—had the greater influence in pointing Kamehameha in a firm direction. He probably derived some positive qualities from each of them.

13 ❧ 'Olohana at Home

After thirty-some years, John Young's life on the high seas ended, and he faced (and was forced to by events) the reality of establishing a landlubber's domicile. As the most experienced sailor of European-style vessels in the region, Young found himself responsible for converting Kamehameha's warriors into fighting sailors and soldiers. This required drilling them both aboard ship and on dry land, over and over again. The former boatswain found himself making frequent use of the shipboard command of "all hands!" summoning the natives to battle stations or to handle an emergency aboard a ship. Soon John Young came to be known by the Hawaiians as 'Olohana. It was as 'Olohana that Young repeatedly drilled the young warriors before taking them into what became the Battle of the Red-Mouthed Gun aboard the *Fair American*. (This was also Young's first experience with an enemy, at least in the Sandwich Islands.)

Such necessities as shelter and sustenance were never a problem for either 'Olohana or Isaac Davis, who were, from the time of their arrival on Hawai'i Island, under the patronage of the high chief Kamehameha. Until 1793 Young resided in a grass house, like everyone else. His was then in Kailua, near the chief's own residence, where Davis had earlier been taken to recover from his wounds. Kailua and its nearby bay were blessed with green vegetation and moderate rainfall, both of which made for pleasant living.

Three years after Hawai'i had become his home, when he had abandoned the idea of escape, Young moved to the hotter and dryer Kawaihae area, thirty-five miles from the cooler coast of Kailua or Kealakekua Bay. There a community of about five hundred Hawaiians lived in grass houses above the beach. Clusters of coconut and banana trees abounded, but there was little more in the way of vegetation at that level. Then, as now, it was not an area renowned for its rainfall. Subsequent visitors, especially sea captains, commented on the less-than-lush land that was Kawaihae. It was cited as barren, arid, often windy, and hardly a sheltered harbor. But apparently the paucity of rain was not a serious problem, for at that time two streams ran from the wooded slopes of Kohala and Waimea. Also, a small spring emptied itself into the bay. The streams carried water until, many years later, the forests were denuded first for sandalwood and fuel for ships' galleys, then by grazing sheep and cattle. Later water diversion for other purposes reduced the flow to Kawaihae considerably.

Desolate as the area may have been to some visitors, the slopes of Kohala, including the upper Kawaihae *ahupua'a* (district), were covered with sandalwood for bartering. Kawaihae staples traded to visiting ships were mostly yams and sweet potatoes, but also included watermelon, cantaloupe, cucumbers, and taro. Quite impressed with the lay of the land, and the abundance of provisions, was Captain John Meares of the *Felice Adventurer*, who wrote in his journal:

From its [Mauna Kea's] base to the sea was a beautiful amphitheater of villages and plantations, while the shore was crowded with people, who, from the coolness of the morning, were clothed in their parti-coloured garments. Some were seated on the banks to look at the ship, while others were running along the shore towards the little sandy patches where their canoes were drawn up, in order to come off to us.

We hove to in the entrance to Toeyah-yah [Kawaihae] Bay which is situated on the Western side of the island, and consequently defended from the violence of the trade winds; nor was it long before a considerable number of canoes came off to the ship with hogs, young pigs, taro root, plantains, sugar-cane and fowls.

Indeed such was the profusion of these articles, that many of the canoes were returned without being able to dispose of their cargoes.[1]

Being very much in the favor of the king, Young had a choice of land and homesites. Two reasons stand out for Young establishing a home in Kawaihae rather than Kailua. Since he had come from a famous seaport city and had sailed the seven seas for about thirty years, he pined for the sea, which may well account for his attempted escape with Davis. Now faced with the reality of a life on land, the seaman in him wanted more than a far-away look at the sea he loved—he wanted to be close to it, to look down to it, and to the distant watery horizon between sky and sea. He longed for the smell of salt air. Kawaihae offered all of that with its high ground only half a mile from the coast. There he established a homestead looking over a panorama of the mightiest sea on the planet. It was a sight any old salt would delight in. It was on this high ground, half a mile from the coast, that there was, between two gulches, a flat ridge. It rose 530 feet above sea level.

On that ridge Young built his domicile. Water ran from the uplands into two gulches on either side of the homesite.

A second reason for Young's decision to locate in Kawaihae was Kamehameha's desire to have him as sort of a business agent for that port with traders and sea captains. Young, with his nautical background and his ability to speak English, was that man for Kamehameha, be he in Kona at his royal residence or his Kawaihae home at Pelekāne by the coast. Young went on the ships, visited with the captains, and learned what cargo was being carried and what could be traded, bought, and sold. When the king was in Kona, Young was carried there by long, swift canoes under sail in four hours. A following European-type vessel might take three or four days. Sometimes Young, at the captain's invitation, sailed with the ship to Kona. Whether Young went on ahead or sailed aboard the ship, he had the opportunity to brief the king on what the ship carried that Kamehameha might want. It was Young who first arranged permission for the ship captains to meet Kamehameha.

John Young's handwriting and signature comprise this receipt dated 1811 for "Three Thousand dollars" for "Tamaahmaa King of the Sandwich Islands." Hawai'i State Archives

Young's lands, all gifts from Kamehameha, amounted to thousands of acres. Many of them owed their productivity to moist uplands and water from the running streams, and of course to the toil of the tenants who lived and labored on the land. His land was known as the *ahupua'a* of Kawaihae Hikina (east). Other lands were later given to Kamehameha's "two foreigners," but the lands were not owned by them in the Western sense of the word. It was the ruling chief, or king, who was the sole and undisputed owner of land divisions on each island. These kings and high chiefs were considered the stewards of the land, for the Hawaiian gods were the true owners. "Because land was immortal and humans mortal, the idea that humans could own land was beyond imagining. Their attitude was one of territorial custody rather than ownership. It was said that land could not belong to men because men belonged to the land."[2]

A parcel of land, or large tracts such as *ahupua'a*, would be assigned to a loyal follower or friend. It was a transaction that could be revoked at the whim of the ruling chief, and often was. Young and Davis were aware that their lands could be reclaimed at any time, but they never were, not by Kamehameha I or by the two sons who succeeded him. It was a situation in which Young could grant land to those whom he considered friends and family, as he did in his will.

While the party to whom the land was "granted" knew that it was revocable, he had all the rights to its produce and the labor of its tenants. Chiefs of *ahupua'a*, as were Young and Davis, did actually control and supervise production and land use, including fishing rights. Seeing that the work was performed, and rents collected, was the task of the *konohiki*, who was in effect a land agent or overseer. His responsibility was to his chief, and on his chief's behalf he made decisions for the best use of the land. The bottom line was, however, that the king was the only one who could dispose of the land, but land was not sold.

While some domestic duties would have been carried out during Young's absence by his wife and older children, the more onerous upkeep of land and food supplies was the work of servants or tenants. When at home, Young would supervise some of the necessary work on the *ahupua'a*, usually by dealing with his *konohiki*. Growing produce was no easy task in an area that often had to depend on rainfall from the misty uplands. Fishing was the job of his servants. Animal husbandry was routine, as was maintenance of the buildings and walls. Young had the first horse on the island, brought in by Captain Richard Cleveland in 1803. He was able to boast that he knew how to ride and care for these animals that so terrified the

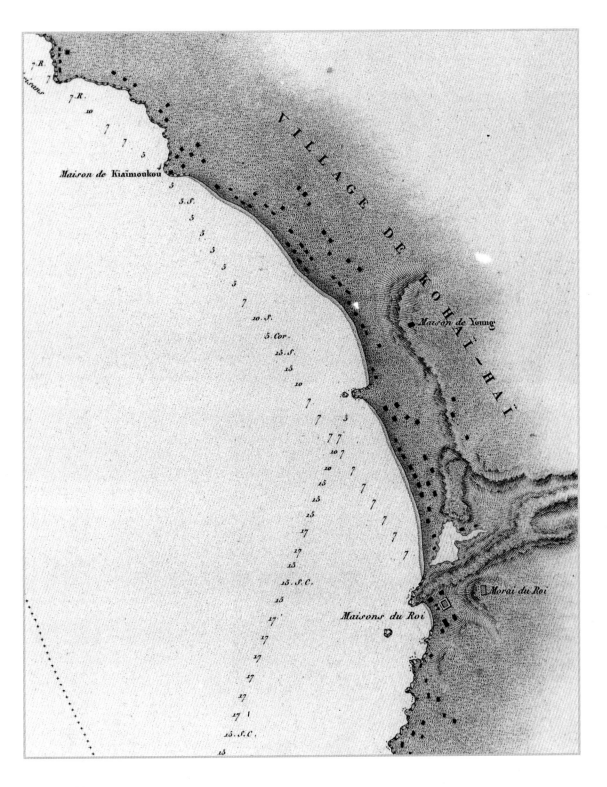

A map of the Kawaihae coastal area by Louis DuPerrey in 1819 included "Maison de Young" (in small type, right center). DuPerrey was an officer and cartographer on the French vessel Uranie *under Captain Louis de Freycinet. Photo courtesy Bishop Museum, Honolulu*

'Olohana at Home

Hawaiians but did not impress Kamehameha. He saw no value in them for conducting land battles, as was the way with European warfare.

In 1812, despite the fact that his battles were over and done with, Kamehameha established a considerable arsenal at Kawaihae in the remains of the old and abandoned Mailekini Heiau. The man Kamehameha entrusted that arsenal to was his competent lieutenant, John Young. Behind its walls were cannon, muskets, swords, and ammunition that had been traded for provisions with numerous visiting ships. Perhaps the only ship captain to refuse to trade arms and ammunition was Vancouver.

It is easy to imagine why Young, when asked by Kamehameha which lands he would like to live upon, would choose the high ground above the Kawaihae Bay. The land granted him was the entire *ahupua'a* of East Kawaihae, which contained thousands of acres rising upward from the coast toward the Kohala mountains and Waimea on the northern slopes of majestic Mauna Kea. The adjacent *ahupua'a*, Komohana (West), was assigned to Kamehameha's prime minister, Kalanimoku. Those Hawaiians who resided on an *ahupua'a* owed allegiance, service, and rents to their landlord. Some servants lived at the homestead, while other workers made their home and living far up the slope of the *ahupua'a* where there were small and scattered communities. Those who were not servants may have paid rent or taxes in the form of fish, hogs, tapa, or rare and prized bird feathers. (It was the *konohiki*'s job, not Young's, to collect taxes and rent.)

In 1793 Young commenced building a home on the lower part of his Kawaihae property on a site about seven hundred feet inland. It was a mix of Hawaiian and Western styles. When, in 1795, Young married a woman by the name of Namokuelua, he had a place they could call home. The young woman had been born on O'ahu in 1780, and it is likely that Young met her after the Battle of O'ahu and married her on that island. The couple had two boys, Robert and James. Namokuela died in 1804 at the age of twenty-four, during an unspecified epidemic. She was buried in the uplands of Waimea.[3]

Six years before her death, Young, in 1798, built on his higher ground several structures. In his journal he noted:

Have begun four buildings. My house the cook house and storage room the house for the children and tahus [guardians] and near the small temple a house for storage. My house at the small rise below the great temple [Pu'ukoholā] more suitable than the ravine which washes away with the Whymea floods.[4]

His stone houses were the first Western-style dwellings in Hawai'i. Including the buildings in the lower portion, he had about seven in the total complex. Those built in 1798 were of basalt but with roofs of thatch (*pili* grass) and poles. The interior walls were covered with plaster made from burnt coral and when whitewashed gave a pleasant appearance. The "main" house measured twenty-one by thirty-four feet. Apparently it had an upper loft. As was customary among Hawaiians who observed the *kapu*, a separate dwelling was provided for the wife.

Mrs. Laura Judd, a missionary wife, makes reference to both the main structure's loft and the wife's house below. (This was the house for Young's second wife, Kaoanaeha, a niece of Kamehameha.) Mrs. Judd was much more impressed with the latter dwelling. In her 1828 memoir she wrote:

He lived in a dirt adobe house, adorned with old rusty muskets, swords, bayonets and cartridge boxes. He gave us supper of goat's meat and fried taro, served on old pewter plates. . . . We were sent up a rickety flight of stairs to sleep. . . . I was afraid of the wind . . . [so I] got up at midnight, [and] went down to the grass house of Mrs. Young, which was neat and comfortable. She [Kaoanaeha] is a noble woman. She lives in native style, one of the sons is with the king and the daughters are in the train of the princess.[5]

Mrs. Judd's very favorable opinion of Kaoanaeha is supported by that of Otto von Kotzebue. One November the Russian sea captain entertained some of the "principal noblemen, among whom was the brother of the queen, Ka'ahumanu. Young brought his wife with him; she is nearly allied [related] to Tamaahmaah." Von Kotzebue commented on the women in native dress but observed that "Mrs. Young, as the wife of a European, is an exception and dresses in the European fashion, in the most costly Chinese silks. Her pleasing countenance, and her very becoming behaviour . . . made an agreeable impression."[6]

That Young kept animals, probably goats and pigs, is gathered from his notes in his journal that the pens (of stone) were whitewashed "as in Wales." His construction style in house and yard were carried over from memories of Lancashire-style homes. 'Olohana's whitewashed buildings were visible from far out at sea, which accounts for some ship captains' entries that they observed from afar the white stone houses of John Young. Von Kotzebue noted that when his vessel, the *Rurick*, was still at sea off Hawai'i Island, "We now saw Young's settlement of several houses built of white stone, after the European fashion. Surrounded by palm and banana trees; the land has a barren appearance."[7] Adelbert von Chamisso noted in 1817: "From far out at sea we could see the European built houses of John Young towering above the grass shacks of the natives."[8] A decade earlier Isaac Iselin had recorded: "We soon went to Mr. Young's habitation, where he entertained us most hospitably during most of the night. . . . Mr. Young occupies several stone buildings , which are the best, (save those of the King, built on the same plan) I have seen on this island."[9] The homestead was occupied well into the middle of the 1800s (fifteen years after Young's death), and nothing indicates it was anything but a happy home, aside from the death of Young's first wife in 1804 and perhaps the deaths of two infants.

The Young family compound as envisioned by artist Herb Kawainui Kāne, based on structural remains and studies carried out by the National Park Service. Little remains today of Young's stone and mortar dwelling, possibly the first Western-style house in the Islands. His wife, children, and servants probably occupied native-style houses nearby. Illustrated are: (A) Young's main house; (B) storage house; (C) possibly Mrs. Young's house; (D) possibly an open-sided thatched work shelter; (E) small native structure, possibly a guardhouse; (F) possibly the cookhouse. Courtesy National Park Service

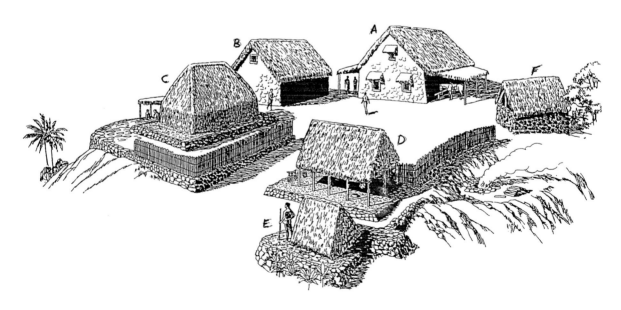

Young's second marriage, to Kaoanaeha, was to a woman with royal lineage. It is she whom Laura Judd described as "a noble woman" in her visit to the homestead. Other visitors have described her as beautiful, not an unusual description of a Hawaiian woman.

Kaoanaeha bore her husband four children: Fanny Kakelaokalani, Grace Kama'iku'i, Keoni Ana (John Jr.), and Jane Lahilahi. (See Young family tree, Appendix IV). Together, with Namokuelua's two young boys, there were many individuals, including servants, making their home in the compound.

Laura Judd may have been one of the few women to have visited the Young homestead, but foreign ships' captains were welcomed under the roof. More often Young visited the vessels and often stayed overnight, even traveling with them to Kailua if the king was there. It was Captain von Kotzebue who revealed that Young was the custodian of mail received by Kamehameha:

I paid a visit to Mr. Young, who gave me to read the letter from King George to Tamaahmaah, the same which Mr. Wilcox had brought from Port Jackson. It was written in the English language, and Tamaahmaah was styled "His Majesty.". . . All the letters which he receives are given to the care of Mr. Young, who possesses the particular confidence of the king, as well as of the people.[10]

The existence of any such letters is not known.

One captain who visited Young's home was Captain Louis de Freycinet of the French ship *Uranie*, who came in 1819. In his account of visiting Young and other chiefs he wrote:

I went out with the intention of paying a visit to the respectable Englishman, Mr. Young, who for such a long time was a friend and counselor of King Tamehameha. The house of this interesting old man [Young was then seventy-two] was located on the top of a small hill which overlooks the village of Kohaihai, it is built of stone, well ventilated, and sanitary. I found him sitting at the foot of his bed, for he had been ill for some time, the death of the king had affected him considerably. He had shared in some way, with him, the supreme power; a favor which made him more than one enemy, and much jealousy.[11]

Another important foreign visitor was the renowned Reverend William Ellis, the energetic and well-educated English missionary out of the London Missionary Society. Ellis had spent some time in Tahiti and the Marquesas, and when he arrived in Hawai'i in 1822 he had a good working knowledge of the Polynesian tongue and customs. His observations and writings on Hawaiian traditions, language, religion, and geography remain a textbook for scholars and researchers pursuing Hawai'i's history and customs of the early part of the nineteenth century. He made it a point to visit John Young, then about seventy-five years old.[12] He noted: "We were kindly received by Mr. Young." Ellis also recorded that Young had rendered the most important service

to the late king; not only in his various civil wars, but in all his intercourse with those foreigners who have visited the islands. I found him recovering from a fit of illness, received from him a cordial welcome, and as he was just sitting down to his morning repast, joined him, with pleasure at his frugal board.[13]

The missionary was grateful to Young for a Sabbath service that at first seemed out of the question. Ellis wrote:

After visiting the temple [Pu'ukoholā] and the king's sacred house I was informed that a vessel would sail for Kairua that evening, a circumstance I much regretted as I hoped to spend the Sabbath at Towaihae. Mr. Young, however, collected his family, and neighbors, to the number of sixty. A short exhortation was given, and followed by prayer, after which I took leave of my kind host.[14]

Further instances of Young's hospitality, as experienced by Ellis, were his warmth and willingness in receiving other traveling members of the missionary party. Ellis noted, among other examples of Young's thoughtfulness, that "Mr. Young furnished a canoe to carry Mr. Thurston back to Kairua."[15] Thurston had preached twice to a Kawaihae gathering.

This is not to imply that the father and husband, John Young, was always present at the homestead, though it was his permanent residence. He often went where his chief went, which was frequently to O'ahu (after the battle of 1795) or to Hilo (near where, in 1796, another important battle was fought). But after 1812 Kamehameha's main base was at Kailua, and

John Young was often there for days at a time. Exceptions were the infrequent occasions when the king and his retinue lived at his royal residence at Kawaihae. It was ringed by coconut trees below the great temple of Puʻukoholā, close to the coast. A stream and a fishpond were close by.

Young's journal contains often repetitive accounts of daily (and minor) Kawaihae happenings, casual observations, and recordings of rents collected. For the most part they are one- or two-liners, frequently containing a brief weather report. Most of the days were "modret," except for "gales and ranes." One day he recorded the "Shock of a earth quake thick fogs and ranes and high tids." Other quakes were sometimes described as alarming. Another day he experienced "small raynes." The items accepted as rent, and perhaps taxes, were often great numbers of pieces of tapa ("tapirs"). "Ded dogs and hogs" are listed among food brought in for rents along with other articles, including much fish. Flying fish, caught in a net, seemed to predominate as the catch of the day. Prized feathers from rare birds, used for decorations on apparel such as cloaks, were sometimes used to pay rent. Young's spelling may not have won him an award, but his penmanship was cursive and clear.

Perhaps Young received the greatest pleasure in noting that "a sale boat was seen and may stop nearby." It would be tantalizing to see a foreign ship, of mysterious origin, on the horizon, only to have it disappear, but it happened more than once. One Thursday he wrote: "There was 2 Rushings Ships at Cona [Kona] but did not learn what they were about nor where they were Bound."

His own comings and goings were seldom mentioned, indicating that he wrote his journal, or diary, while living at the homestead. This is borne out by the fact that most of the contents of the one journal available were written between 1808 and 1809, while the king was on Oʻahu. During those years Young was governor of Hawaiʻi Island, a position he held from 1802 until 1812. It appears that he once went with "Coamoa to Heedo [Hilo] to By a cannow." Another time he made mention of Isaac Davis, but the context is unclear. It was December 1808, two years before the mysterious death of his colleague.

There is a gap from 1809 to 1821, with entries for two months only. The existing journal's final entry, of no consequence, was in 1825. But a significant entry is found for "October Thursday the 11th," the year unknown: "Captn Benat [Bennett] arrived at Toay [Kawaihae] bay from the NW coast got 9 thousand skins The same day saw the ship Erad [Arab] Captn Lues

[Lewis] another brig Thaddeus Capn Blanchard." The latter was the vessel that five years earlier had brought the first company of New England missionaries to Hawai'i. Its first landfall is generally accepted as April 1, 1820, at Kawaihae. (First officer James Hunnewell of the *Thaddeus* puts the date as March 30.) Young's date of Thursday, October 11, for the *Thaddeus* probably refers to its subsequent visits to Kawaihae. Also, there is no documented evidence that Young was at Kawaihae on April 1, 1820, despite what some writers have stated. Hiram Bingham's account tells of arriving in Kailua about four or five days after leaving Kawaihae and then going to the Kailua house of John Young.

Lieutenant Peter Puget, probably at Vancouver's request, had urged Young and Davis to keep, if not a journal, notes pertinent to the life about them:

To both I made such presents as were suited to their Situations & as Young could write he was furnished with Paper, Pens, &c. for that purpose, he promised to observe more minutely their manners Customs &c. than he had hitherto done, which on our next arrival would greatly assist us in the Descriptive part of the Sandwich Islands.[16]

Young may well have kept his promise to Puget, but presumably such notes as he made for the commander of the *Chatham* were lost in a flood that swept away Young's papers.

The appellation "'Olohana" remained with Young until the end. Long after his death, the many who knew of him still thought of him as 'Olohana. Today a street in the center of Waikiki remembers and honors Young with the name 'Olohana. Also, a grandson of Isaac Davis, who later in life became a magistrate in Waimea, was known as 'Olohana.

14 ❧ The Russians Are Coming!

The first significant Russian presence in the central Pacific occurred in 1804 when Captain Urey Lisiansky, commander of the *Neva,* arrived on Hawai'i Island. He first noted that it was governed in the king's absence "by an Englishman with the name of Young."[1] Lisiansky spent twelve days on the island and reported that he learned much about Hawaiian customs and government from Young. He also did a great deal of trading with Young and left with good impressions of the former boatswain.

By the first part of the nineteenth century, the Russian colony of New Archangel was well established in Alaskan waters on what is now Sitka, where a strong Russian culture is still evident. New Archangel was the Pacific base for the Russian trading firm known as the Russian-American Company. (The "American" part of the name comes not from a United States association but relates to fur trading on the North American continent.) Administrator for this pioneer mission was the able seventy-five-year-old Alexander Baranoff, governor of the colony.

The Russians welcomed the opportunity to obtain such necessities as fruit, vegetables, and meat from their Hawai'i neighbors, several thousand miles due south. In fact, it was so convenient that Baranoff conceived a plan to not only establish a base in Hawai'i but to make the islands a colonial outpost.[2] At the very least it would provide a dependable food supply for the Sitka settlers. There was also the strong likelihood of entering the lucrative sandalwood trade.

An opportunity for getting a foothold on that cluster of attractive, fertile, and friendly islands was soon provided. On January 31, 1815, one of Russia's trading vessels, the *Bering,* was wrecked off the island of Kaua'i; its cargo, or part of it, was taken ashore by Kaua'i natives.[3] Baranoff wanted to salvage what he could, or be indemnified by Kaua'i's King Kaumualii for what his people kept for themselves. To accomplish this he sent as his emissary Georg Anton Scheffer, a German doctor who had attached himself to the Baranoff operation, and who already had delusions of grandeur. As history would show, he was an adventurer and an entrepreneur with grandiose ambitions.

The assignment was welcomed by Scheffer, who had visions of

obtaining more than salvaged cargo. The imperialist in him visualized a strong Russian presence in the Sandwich Islands, which had been united into a kingdom only five years earlier. He contemplated the overthrow of its ruler, Kamehameha, with the aid of the Russians, and placing Kaumualii on the king's throne under Russian protection. Salvage matters aside, Scheffer and the Kaua'i king had a common interest in becoming a power structure under a Russian flag, and leaving Kamehameha to worry about what came next. However, Scheffer, a wily diplomat (some called him cunning), made it a point to visit Kamehameha at Kailua, where he won the king over by posing primarily as a professional naturalist. He also won over the royal court, and before long he had not only been given storehouse space in Honolulu for trading, but also generous gifts of prime land. All this happened despite words of caution from John Young to his king, for he sensed something sinister in the glib-tongued agent for Baranoff. Scheffer even managed, in 1815, to commence construction of a small blockhouse near Honolulu Harbor. It would serve little purpose as a fortification per se, but it did fly the Russian flag for upwards of a year.

Back on Kaua'i, the Russian emissary ingratiated himself with Kaumualii by infusing in him the dream of being once again a sovereign in his own right instead of ruling under the shadow of Kamehameha, as he had done since their negotiated peace in 1810. Kaumualii gladly signed agreements, marked with an X, drawn up by Scheffer, which were designed to favor the Russians as more than visitors. The German doctor had no problem being granted permission to build for the Russians a substantial fort at Waimea, on Kaua'i's western shore. It was a formidable installation in every respect, and it signaled Russia's intention to remain on Kaua'i, at the same time looking toward the southern islands of Hawai'i. It was named Fort Elisabeth, in honor of the czarina, though neither she nor her royal spouse may have been aware of it. It occupied over two acres of land and had at least thirty-five gun positions (with guns in place). The walls were from fifteen to thirty feet thick, and the magazine was protected by a substantial casement. The Russian flag flew bravely over Fort Elisabeth, as it did over the blockhouse at Honolulu, but both flew without sanction from St. Petersburg.

At the same time that Kaua'i's western shores were being "protected," Scheffer discovered the idyllic beauty of Kaua'i's Hanalei Valley and its splendid beaches. Not only did Kaumualii grant him permission to build another, though smaller, fort there, but he was generous in giving him handsome acreage in the wooded and fertile valley. The fort was named

Fort Alexander, after the czar. Here, too, the flag bearing the two-headed Russian eagle flew from the wall facing the sea. Russian guns were mounted on the Hanalei heights, also directed to the sea.

To Kaumualii, not all that pleased at being a subordinate of Kamehameha, Scheffer's plan for a Russian occupation of Kaua'i and half of O'ahu (which Kaumualii claimed belonged to him) sounded promising. Encouraged by Kaumualii, the entrepreneur went back to Honolulu to negotiate with Kamehameha and nail down some of his demands for Russian territorial occupation. Meanwhile, the tide had turned, for John Young and some Yankee traders saw Scheffer for what he was, an emissary without a portfolio.

Perhaps most daunting to Scheffer was the sizable Honolulu fort, which had been built under the supervision of John Young and at the command of Kamehameha, who had since had a change of heart. As governor of O'ahu at the time, Young's authority allowed him to recruit all able-bodied males from the four quarters of O'ahu. Construction of the fort commenced in January 1816 and lasted most of the year. Its measurements were 340 feet by 300 feet, and its walls ranged from twenty feet at the base to twelve feet at the top. It was made mostly of adobe with facings outside and inside of coral rocks from the nearby reef. From forty to fifty guns occupied prominent placements. Its entrance faced the mountains, and from this Fort Street, still a historical thoroughfare in downtown Honolulu, got its name. Built for Honolulu's protection, the fort was a visible threat to unwelcome intruders or designers. It was located in the area now bounded by Aloha Tower and the foot of Bishop Street.

Adelbert von Chamisso, a bona-fide German naturalist traveling with von Kotzebue, was not impressed with the fort's structure and its effectiveness in repulsing any invaders. Wrote this foreign observer:

The fort in the background of the harbour of Hana-rura, which Mr. Young had erected without judgment, is merely a square of dry brick wall, without bastions or towers, and without ditches, and does not answer the double interior of the Governor [king], to defend himself against external attack and an internal enemy. The fort ought to be regularly built where it now stands, and there ought to be a battery on the external edge of the reef, to defend the entrance to the harbour.[4]

Not withstanding Chamisso's call for a fort of European propor-

The Honolulu fort, built in 1816 under the order of Kamehameha. John Young, then governor of Oʻahu, supervised its construction. Hawaiian Historical Society, Honolulu

Troops training inside the Honolulu fort. Hawaiian Historical Society, Honolulu

tions and design, such as to defend the gateway to the Rhine, Young's fort served its purpose. It intimidated and threatened. Scheffer was confident enough to return from O'ahu to Kaua'i, where he spent much of 1816 mending his fences and counting his profits before they hatched.[5] Much to his chagrin, the expected Baranoff blessing did not materialize. From where he sat in his New Archangel headquarters, Baranoff learned of the difficulties Scheffer was encountering and now wanted no part of the scheme. Nor did he feel that his imperial government would object to the abandonment of such a plan as had been initiated. In fact, Scheffer's expansion plan for Russia never did have imperial diplomatic approval. Before the three-year debacle had ended, both Baranoff and the czar repudiated Scheffer and his actions.

When Kamehameha learned of Scheffer's quiet and subversive invasion plans, he sent chiefs to Kaumualii with an order to expel the Russians from that island. The Russians resisted and had to be forced out, but out they went. It was the end of the threat of uninvited visitors flying a foreign flag. Much credit for the failure of the Russian adventure goes to Governor Baranoff, who, when he learned of Scheffer's plans and progress, terminated any agreement between them.[6] Kaumualii also terminated the agreements he had signed with Scheffer, over strong objections from the German.

Von Kotzebue's visit to Hawai'i in 1818 was the year after, by royal Hawaiian command, the Russians folded their tents and were forced out of Kaumualii's domain. When von Kotzebue met Kamehameha he made it quite clear that his government had no knowledge of a Russian desire to take any part of the islands, for trade or occupation. It was then that von Kotzebue learned that the Hawaiians had been very apprehensive of the earlier Russian presence, and now they were apprehensive of his own vessel and crew. It was only when Young intervened that their fears were quieted, and that von Kotzebue and the *Rurick* were accepted as an exploratory expedition on a peaceful visit. Von Kotzubue wrote that John Young, "one of the principal confidants of the king . . . was sent to Woahoo to build the fort. His adventures are well-known from Vancouver's voyages."[7]

One compelling reason for Baranoff to distance himself from Scheffer's proprietary interest in Hawai'i was Baranoff's belief that the Sandwich Islands were under the protection of England, as "ceded" by Kamehameha through Vancouver.[8] Czar Alexander I was of a similar mind, and he instructed the Russian-American Company to confine itself "to the maintenance of peaceful commercial relations with the islands."[9] The Russian eagle flew north from Hawai'i and did not return.

Repudiated by Baranoff, and later the czar himself, Scheffer went to Honolulu after being forced from Kaua'i, but from there he was told to be gone, and now.[10] He soon found his way to Canton. From there it is reported that he went to St. Petersburg, where he would have received no welcome, particularly from the czar. It is reported that Scheffer traveled to Brazil and again did well for himself in the acquisition of fine lands and the favor of Emperor Don Pedro. But that adventure also went awry and he returned to his native Germany, where he died on his estate in 1836, far from the southern islands than might have been annexed to Russia had he been more of a diplomat than a dictator.

The fort that John Young had constructed, and which was commanded by Captain George Beckley (another Englishman in the service of Kamehameha), had served its purpose. It had intimidated a likely invader, and possibly others who looked longingly at the Sandwich Islands for their strategic setting and ample supply of provisions. Before its demise in 1857, it served as a prison for local and foreign transgressors. It also gained an infamous name for itself as the "holding cell" for numerous recalcitrant Hawaiian Catholics, who in violation of the Protestant edict issued by Queen Ka'ahumanu not to practice their faith, were imprisoned. Aside from serving as a place of incarceration, court cases were frequently held there. Until its usefulness was over, it still "provided a healthy moral influence over the port and the town."[11]

Back in St. Petersburg, Czar Alexander, though he repudiated the Russian adventure in Hawai'i, wished to remain on good terms with his nearest Hawaiian neighbor, the king of Kaua'i. To that end, and as a gesture of good will, the czar had a gold medal struck, reading, "To Tomari [Kaumualii], chief of the Sandwich Islands, in recognition of his friendship with the Russians."[12] In addition, he ordered that the king be given a beautiful mounted sword and a scarlet cloak with lace and tassels. For reasons unknown to historians, these gifts were never delivered to the Kaua'i king.

15 ❖ Royal Rite of Passage

The young Kamehameha was famed not only for his muscular and well-proportioned body, but also for his prowess in wrestling and other sports enjoyed by young Hawaiian males. He had all the requisites for a virile and superb warrior. He was accomplished in the martial arts, having trained as a youth under the master Kekūhaupiʻo. "His strength," wrote Kamakau, "lay in his shoulders, which were broad and muscular, and in his back. Until the year he died he had the reputation of being among the best surfboard riders in the islands. His powerful jaws showed energy and determination of character."[1] He excelled in throwing the spear, a weapon as common as it was dangerous. Vancouver was once witness to a military demonstration of combat skills among a group of manly Hawaiians. Kamehameha, then in his mid-forties, ordered his "opponents" to hurl six blunt spears at him, all at the same time. Two he caught, three he parried, and the other he dodged.[2] As he did in his exhibition with the spears, he fought, dodged, and parried in many a battle and skirmish during his life, and escaped unscathed from each.

In his later years he remained healthy not only in body but in mind, the latter perhaps because he could relax from warring, now that Kauaʻi had been gained by peaceful means. He remained under the mistaken notion that his kingdom was under the protection of his good friend, Great Britain. This may have given him courage when it became evident that Scheffer's designs, if successful, would subject him to Russian rule.

Visitors—for the most part friendly traders from foreign ports—increased as Westerners became more exploratory. Kamehameha remained cordial to them, continuing to accept the counsel of his chief and advisor, John Young. In addition to accepting Young's input, he also accepted a variety of foreign gifts. Quite often these consisted of European apparel, likely as not either nautical wear or garments that represented a national royalty. Vancouver had given him three ornate cloaks (though none would be nearly so rare and valuable as the yellow-feathered cloak that the king alone possessed). The Prince Regent of England in 1812 sent him a tri-

*Kamehameha at Kamakahonu, a cove near Kailua-Kona, where the king
resided after the wars were over. At the left are two ladies of the court, and
across the cove is the king's private temple. The fish represent food brought daily
to the court. In conversation with his son Liholiho, Kamehameha is depicted*

wearing a simple kapa *garment. With him are his prime minister and
other court attendants. In his last years Kamehameha ruled as a just and
benevolent monarch, often in counsel with John Young.* © *Herb Kawainui Kāne.*
Collection of King Kamehameha Hotel, Kailua-Kona, Hawai'i

cornered hat, complete with plumes. It was accompanied by a red-cloth full-dress uniform, its edges embroidered in gold.[3]

From Governor Baranoff, on behalf of the Russian-American Company, came a scarlet cloak, a blue coat, and gray trousers. By this time such regalia were no longer a novelty to the king. Archibald Campbell observed that after trying on the Russian garment, "he gave it to his attendants to be taken to shore. I never saw him wear it again."[4] Even more elaborate was the Russian uniform for a naval staff officer. It was green with a gold collar and gold frogs. The suggestion was made by Baranoff, through Scheffer, that Kamehameha wear it at public gatherings, and especially upon the arrival of Russian and other foreign vessels. There is no indication that the suggestion was ever implemented, perhaps because Kamehameha sensed the symbolism that such a uniform might convey to other nations.

Louis Choris, the artist and draftsman on von Kotzebue's ship, the *Rurick,* recorded:

I asked Tammeamea permission to do his portrait; this prospect pleased him very much, but he asked me to leave him alone an instant, so he could dress. Imagine my surprise on seeing this monarch display himself in the costume of a sailor; he wore blue trousers, a red waistcoat, a clean white shirt and a necktie of yellow silk. I begged him to change his dress; he refused absolutely and insisted on being painted just as he was.[5]

Choris had two sittings with the sovereign in a sailor's suit, one in the morning at first dawn, another in the afternoon, at which von Kotzebue was present. The afternoon sitting was less than satisfactory both to the artist and the subject. Perhaps Kamehameha was restless and tired from the morning. Von Kotzebue wrote: "Mr. Choris succeeded admirably well in taking his likeness, although Tammeamea to make it more difficult would not sit still for a moment, but was making grimaces all the time."[6]

When the ordeal was over, there were details for Choris to decide about Kamehameha's portrait being combined with that of a female head. The matter was put to John Young to decide. Young was on Oʻahu at the time and there the *Rurick* found him. He had reservations about the combination of the two artworks, and his advice to separate the two figures was accepted.[7]

It was ironic that, as Kamehameha aged, such a survivor in battle should fall victim to an undiagnosed ailment. He had even survived the fatal cholera epidemic of 1803, which carried away many of his chiefs and hardy warriors. During the winter of 1818–19 a wave of influenza swept through the islands, and both Kamehameha and Ka'ahumanu may have come down with it. Whether the king was felled by that or another illness, we know only from Kamakau that "he was a long time ill."[8]

When Captain Golovnin saw the king in the last year of his life, he observed:

He is still strong, active, temperate and sober. He does not use liquor or eat to excess. We can see in him a combination of childishness and ripe judgment. Some of his acts would do credit to a more enlightened ruler. His honesty and love of justice have been shown in many cases.[9]

The Russian navigator went on to comment that what petty faults the "old king had they would not obscure his merits."[10]

When word of Kamehameha's illness spread, many of his chiefs who were on O'ahu gathering sandalwood were summoned back to Kailua. At the outset he was treated by such men as Kua'ua'u, Kalanimoku, Kuaka-mauna, and others who had attended to him before and were experts in the medicinal arts. When the illness would not yield to their treatment, a ship was sent to Honolulu for Don Francisco de Paula Marin, merchant, agron-omist, friend of Kamehameha, and one who had some medical knowledge. Though the Spaniard remained four days, until the king's death, his Euro-pean knowledge of medicine was no more effective than native prayers and practices. Kamakau writes that it was then that Kuakamauna told Kame-hameha: "The doctors have done all they can, you must place yourself in the hands of the god who alone has power over life and death." It was at this point that a human sacrifice was called for, perhaps as a way of propitiating the appropriate god. But Kamehameha, whose faculties remained with him until the end, objected, exclaiming that "men are sacred to the chief," a ref-erence to his son and heir, Liholiho.[11]

It is correct to say that Kamehameha was a very religious person. He was religious in observing the many *kapu* that dictated, defined, and pre-scribed Hawaiian day-to-day living, including eating—especially eating, for men and women were forbidden to sit down and eat together. The *kapu* were also observed before and during battle. He had always seen to it that the privileges of the chiefs and the *kapu* were strictly observed. According to Daws, "Kamehameha had begun his pursuit of power as one of the many chiefs bound by the sacred rituals of the *kapu* system; he ended as an absolute king who could make rituals work for him. The *kapu* served his needs admirably."[12] The rites and customs he lived by were ancient, and they were respected and practiced by way of prayer and obedience, sacrifice and worship. They embraced almost all aspects and activities of all classes of the Hawaiian people. Kamehameha had remained faithful to the *kapu* in life, and he remained so as death closed in.

According to Kamakau, Vancouver was impressed with Kamehameha's observance of religious practices. "You are a religious chief, Kamehameha, and you worship wooden images," said Vancouver.[13] But his endeavor to get the king to accept Christianity was unsuccessful. Perhaps because Vancouver saw how devoted Kamehameha was to his gods, he did not encourage the sending of missionaries from Great Britain. Nor were other foreign visitors any more successful in persuading the king to abandon his ancient faith and deeply held traditions for the Christian teachings.[14] His answer to Vancouver, who tried to win him over, was recorded by Captain Ebenezer Townsend:

The king Amma-amma-hah told Capt. Vancouver that he would go with him on to the high mountain Mona Roah [Mauna Loa] and they would both jump off together, each calling on their separate gods for protection, and if Capt. Vancouver's god saved him, but himself was not saved, then his people would believe as Capt. Vancouver did.[15]

There is no record of the challenge being accepted.

At the time of his death, Kamehameha was not about to abandon the gods who had stood by him in life. As his condition worsened, religious services, ceremonies, and prayers from the *kahuna* were the order of the day. John Young was there to witness the incantations, the attempts of a medical cure, and the praying. "The supplications to Kamehameha's god Ka'ili and to the sorcery gods, Pua and Kapo, were ineffective."[16] Toward the evening of May 7, 1819, the king took a morsel of food and a swallow of water. He had neither strength nor desire for more. When asked by one of the chiefs standing near the bedside to say something, Kamehameha said nothing. Then, relates Kamakau, chief Kaikioewa asked him for a last word, perhaps to give them an instruction. He told his king, "We are all here, your younger brothers, your chiefs, your foreigner [John Young]. Give us a word." The words the dying king gave to the small but prestigious group were, "Endless is the good that I have given you to enjoy." Kamakau tells us that "then John Young put his arms around his neck and kissed him."[17] Actually, Young touched the nose of his dying friend and sovereign. The Hawaiian word *honi* signifies salutation, nose touching, or nose rubbing.

A slightly different version is recounted by the missionary Hiram Bingham, who was not present. In answering the chiefs' request for "your charge for us" the dying king made an effort, but being unable to finish his sentence, "embraced the neck of the foreigner and drew him down for a kiss."[18] Historian James T. Pole says that "he raised his arm and drew down John Young's head to touch noses in a last farewell."[19] It was his last act of aloha. To high chief Hoapili, in his last breath, he whispered his wishes for disposition of his remains. He expired about two hours before dawn on May 8, 1819. If he was born in 1753, then the great Kamehameha died at the age of sixty-six. John Young, one of the last men to bid Kamehameha good-bye, had a brotherly relationship with the king that was surely one of the strangest alliances of the day—a Lancashire sailor and a monarch of the Hawaiian Islands.

As he had been in life, in death the king was revered and worshipped by his many followers. Weeping and despair overcame his people when they

John Young visits the dying Kamehameha.
Illustration by Herb Kawainui Kāne. Collection of the author

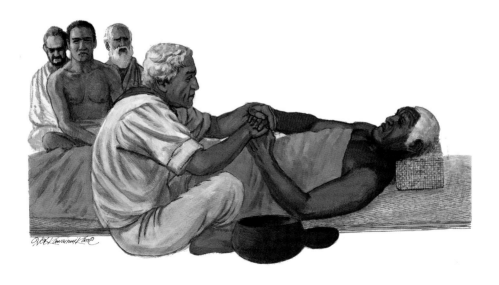

learned of their king's passing. As was the custom when an important Hawaiian died, violent exhibitions of grief took place. Now all restraints were cast aside, "as if their world was ending. Drunken frenzies, tearing of clothes and knocking out the front teeth were among the displays of their grief."[20]

Shortly after his father's death the new king, Liholiho, left Kailua to escape the anticipated defilement of death. He and some of his followers went to Kawaihae and remained there for several days. In keeping with custom, only the bones of the dead were kept. Kamehameha's body was taken to the nearby *heiau* for final disposition by the priests. First the body was washed, then wrapped in a shroud of green taro and banana leaves. It was then placed in a prepared trench, covered with earth, where a fire was built and kept burning for about ten days. Then the flesh was scraped from the bones and buried at sea.[21]

Meanwhile, rituals of prayer and lengthy incantations filled the days and nights as the *kahuna* and the people observed the *kapu* associated with the final rites of a great chieftain. The final disposition of the bones was more sacred and secretive. A special basketlike container called a *ka'ai*, tightly woven of sennet, was fashioned. The king's bones were encased in it for carrying to the final resting place. According to Dorothy Barrere, who drew upon Kamakau, "the ka'ai was taken by the chief Ho'olulu to Kaloko in North Kona, to be deposited in a secret cave there under the direction of the high chief Ulumaheihei Hoapili and the sacred chiefess Keōpūolani."[22] The site of the secret cave where the great king's bones came to rest remains unknown. Even now the Hawaiians say, as did their forefathers and those before them, "the morning star alone knows where Kamehameha's bones are guarded."[23]

It should be noted that Kamehameha is one of the two individuals chosen to represent Hawai'i in the statuary Hall of Fame of our nation's capitol (the other is Blessed Damien de Veuster).

16 ❧ The Coming of the Calvinists

Aside from the arrival of the Westerners with Captain Cook, there is perhaps no more historic day in the annals of Hawai'i, for better or worse, than April 1, 1820. It was then, after a 164-day voyage from Boston, that the brig *Thaddeus,* with Captain Andrew Blanchard, bound for the Sandwich Islands, made its first Hawaiian landfall at Kawaihae.[1] On board, besides Blanchard, were First Officer James Hunnewell, eleven men (four of whom were young Hawaiians, including George Kaumualii, the son of Kaua'i's King Kaumualii), seven women (wives of the seven missionaries), and five Chamberlain children.[2] The adults were ordained and lay missionaries of the American Board of Commissioners of Foreign Missions (ABCFM). Their immediate and long-range goal was to save the heathen Hawaiians from themselves and from sin.

This Pioneer Company, as it was known, was the first of twelve companies that the ABCFM would send to Hawai'i over the next twenty-seven years. All the missionary men and women had been trained at Cornwall Foreign Mission School in Connecticut. The four Hawaiian young men who were returning home had been helpers at the school. The missionary band was ready to do battle with Satan in the Sandwich Islands. Five of the men were ordained ministers. Twenty-nine-year-old Elisha Loomis was a printer who would soon be at work with his printing press and type. Another nonminister, but a missionary nonetheless, was Thomas Holman, a physician who was a medical school graduate and had also studied at the Cornwall Foreign Mission School. The carpenter and farmer Daniel Chamberlain was "to teach the natives agriculture and the mechanical arts."[3]

The acknowledged leader (some said self-anointed) of this First Company was the Reverend Hiram Bingham, who with his wife remained in Hawai'i in a leadership capacity for two decades. During those years Bingham became a powerful influence on the Hawaiian way of life. He, with the many missionaries who followed, had much to say not only on spiritual matters, but also about the educational and political affairs of the small nation. In doing so, Bingham left himself subject to criticism, not only by Hawaiians who found him overly zealous, but also by the Catholic missionaries who came in 1827 and the Mormons who entered the field in 1850.

Both of the latter religious groups were frowned upon by the American missionaries as outright intruders. It was a matter of holy competition, and Bingham held his ground by engaging the strong support of Queen Regent Ka'ahumanu, as well as by putting the educational school system under the aegis of the Protestant missionaries. He had clearly deviated from the very specific instructions given to the Pioneer Company by the Boston-based ABCFM. The instructions were not only clear and concise, they were laudable in their concern for the Hawaiian people. They have also been described as ethnocentric and perhaps a bit condescending. They read in part:

Your views are not to be limited to the low, narrow scale, but you are to open your hearts wide and set your goals high. You are to aim at nothing short of covering these islands with fruitful fields, and pleasant dwellings and schools and churches, and of raising up the whole people to an elevated state of Christian civilization. You are to obtain an adequate language of the people; to make them acquainted with letters, to give them the Bible, with skill to read it, . . . to introduce and get into extended operation and influence among them, the arts and institutions and usages of civilized life and society; and you are to abstain from all interference with local and political interests of the people and to inculcate the duties of justice, moderation, forbearance, truth and universal kindness. Do all in your power to make men of every class good, wise and happy.[4]

Bingham has been faulted in particular for his often deep involvement in the political affairs of the national and local governments. He openly disregarded the admonition to abstain from political affairs, and thus for a number of years Calvinism was Hawai'i's state religion, vigorously enforced by the convert queen, Ka'ahumanu. Bingham's role would cause much upheaval at high levels and even disagreement among his colleagues. His assertiveness in mixing matters of God and government did not reflect the views of all his fellow preachers. Before his twenty years of service ended he was not, by virtue of his strict Calvinist conformity, a beloved leader. "A few of his countrymen at the Islands conceded that he had done some good, though they wished God had called him to do it somewhere else."[5]

But it was Bingham who would be the first of the company to set foot on Kawaihae beach, and to be greeted by the young King Liholiho's premier, Kalanimoku, who was also at that time the leading resident chief. Bingham writes in his autobiography that he made a visit to the great temple Puʻukoholā with Kalanimoku. Most important was the news of Kamehameha's death, translated for Bingham by the Hawaiians who had been on the ship and who served as competent interpreters. Equally startling, and surely pleasing to the missionary company, was news that this new king, Kamehameha's son, had overthrown many of the *kapu*, destroyed temples and idols, and in general created a religious void. John Young, who as a major statesman took part in many changes within the islands, is credited with having joined in destruction of the *kapu* of 1819.[6] The overthrow of the centuries-old traditions and religious practices was not without repercussions. The older and more conservative chiefs and their followers rebelled. Battles were fought, and friends became enemies. In the end the traditionalists were defeated, and a new way of life was underway even before the arrival of the missionaries.

Aside from the scuttling of the *kapu*, there was court revelry as well as discontent among the chiefs who resented what they considered the invasion of "Americans, Englishmen, Frenchmen and Russians. . . . It was John Young, able counselor to Kamehameha, who kept the kingdom together during these crucial months."[7] The level-headed Young, along with Kalanimoku, persuaded Liholiho to curb the festivities and to convene a general council to deal with gnawing problems.

The missionaries could not have arrived at a time more advantageous to their purpose. What they found was a vacuum; a ship of state minus its religious rudder. Surely this had been divined and designed by the hand of the Almighty! All these glad tidings Bingham learned before the *Thaddeus* departed Kawaihae for Kailua, where it arrived on April 4. Nowhere does Bingham make mention of John Young being present at the Kawaihae landing or the visit to the temple, though some writers have said, others implied, that Young was present to welcome the missionaries. Nor does Young mention it in his diary, though several months later he records seeing the *Thaddeus*, presumably on one of its subsequent trips to Hawaiʻi Island.

At the time that Bingham arrived at Kawaihae, Young was at his Kailua residence, where Liholiho and his court resided. It was there, on about April 4 or 5, that Bingham found the "foreigner." The missionary leader recorded that "we went to the house of John Young."[8] It was wise of Bingham and his close associates to go to Young's Kailua home. (They were soon appalled that he had married a native woman.)

Apparently their first meeting with Liholiho was less than satisfactory; nothing was resolved, though missionary credentials and gifts were presented. Soon a council meeting was held, and John Young was, as a chief, a very important part of it. Bingham wrote: "Though he did not object to the landing of the missionaries . . . he feared the rivalry might grow between United States and Great Britain, which at the time was supposed to hold a protectorate over the kingdom."[9] Young's fears were groundless; nothing happened in that respect. But the situation indicated that Young, like Kamehameha, considered Hawai'i, at least the island, under the protection of Great Britain.

The missionaries, after explaining their purpose and requesting to settle in the islands, left some of the chiefs in favor of their mission, while others expressed doubts. The king himself was quite uncertain. An impasse existed. The missionaries despaired of having to wait weeks or even months for a reply, meanwhile living in the cramped quarters of their sailing ship offshore. As the missionaries bit their nails while the king and his chiefs were in deliberation, James Hunnewell visited Young, who like himself, hoped for a decision. Hunnewell wrote:

John Young to me, professed to be very glad that the missionaries had come among them to preach and to teach. He had got down his old Bible, brushed the dust off, and I saw him reading it on my visit to his house, while awaiting action of the Council of Chiefs, then assembled at Kailua.[10]

It was Chief John Young who provided a temporary solution:

Speaking to the king and the court Young declared "These kahunas worship the same God as those of our country of whom Vancouver said to Kamehameha 'When I go back to Great Britain let me ask King George to send you kahunas.' Let the chiefs try them out by permitting them to remain in Hawai'i for a year; then if you discover they are not doing right, let the chiefs send them away."[11]

A similar version was documented by an unknown author, who was likely one of the first missionaries:

When they arrived they went first to Liholiho and his counselors to talk about a place to stay. Some of the chiefs were doubtful [about allowing this] because of Vancouver's having said to Kamehameha that upon his return he would send priests from Britain. And because of their doubt, there was much discussion between the chiefs and the missionaries—for five days perhaps, the discussion lasted. Because of this a haole [foreigner] from England who had formerly lived with Kamehameha on Hawai'i, 'Olohana by name said, "The kahuna of Britain and those of America are the same, their prayers are the same; they have one God; they do not have different Gods."[12]

The authors of the *Thaddeus* journal recorded that a solution to any problem with Great Britain could be handled by the involvement of John Young. They wrote:

To obviate what seemed to be an objection, the fear of displeasing Great Britain, they concluded that Mr. Young should write to England to inform the people that American missionaries had come to settle here, not to do any harm, but to teach the people of these Islands all good things.[13]

There is no record that John Young ever wrote such a letter, nor was there a need for him to do so. On November 27, 1826, a letter in John Young's name testified to "the great and radical change already made for the better" (see Appendix II). However, the composition is not the work of John Young—it is not his language. Bingham or one of his luminaries saw the value of a testimonial from Young, one they would write and he would sign. Undoubtedly, Young could concur with the contents. The missionaries could, and later did, credit Young for this respite. The missionary Lorenzo Lyons noted several years later that "Mr. Young was the only foreigner who favored the coming of the missionaries, and he has been kind to them ever since."

The suggestion for a period of probation was accepted. Days later the majority of the missionaries sailed for O'ahu, which, as Liholiho noted, was where "most white men seemed to prefer." Only the Thurstons and Holmans remained on Hawai'i Island. Whether any serious monitoring was implemented to see if the missionaries were "doing right" is unrecorded. They had arrived in Hawai'i and in Hawai'i they stayed. Whether they should have ever come still provides apt and sometimes argumentative discussion in Hawai'i today, almost 180 years after their arrival. It has been regarded as a strange coincidence that Kamehameha should die at Kailua and the missionaries should land at this same place, all within a year. It was good fortune for the missionaries that they found Young at that same place.

17 ✦ Character References

The mark and memory of a man, and a woman, is often determined by the opinion of those who personally knew the individual. Frequently, those opinions are short lived. Other times, depending upon the person with an opinion and the temper of those times, testimonials favorable to an individual may be perpetuated. The deeds and actions by which a person may be well remembered become part of the tapestry.

Many threads have woven a picture of John Young as his little-known life becomes more exposed. Numerous testimonials are found among the journals of ship officers with whom Young had contact, usually on behalf of Kamehameha. Captain George Vancouver's opinions, cited earlier, leave no doubt about his admiration for both Young and Davis. The great navigator said of both, "They have been materially instrumental in causing the excellent relations we have had with the inhabitants."[1] Vancouver continued:

Young and Davis bid us farewell with a degree of reluctance that did credit to their feelings. . . . Their behavior on the island has been meritorious in the highest sense of the word, supporting by their character (for they possessed nothing else) such a degree of consequences, that while it insured them respect, it engaged the affections and regard, of the natives; and of no one more than the king himself who did not fail to listen to their counsel and advices and I am well persuaded we had been much indebted for our very friendly and hospitable reception; as also for the orderly and civil behavior we experienced from the inhabitants, by their attention to the instructions and examples of these our countrymen.[2]

Clearly the two former subjects of Great Britain impressed Vancouver, so much so that he advised Kamehameha to "not permit foreigners to settle in Hawai'i. Two only should stay. 'Olohana and 'Aikake [Davis]. Most of the foreigners are men of very bad character. . . . They will lead you astray."[3] Vancouver concluded by stating that since Young and Davis "might be encouraged to continue in the exercise of these virtuous principles which they had taught, I gave them a written testimonial of their good conduct, and in the most serious manner enjoined them to persevere in that path that their own good understanding has pointed."[4] High praise indeed from Vancouver, who had, by virtue of his heavy responsibilities, been a good judge of men.

Peter Puget, commander of the *Chatham* at the time of Vancouver's third visit, wrote:

> *I was much pleased to find everyone to Speak well of Young and Davis. [Kamehameha] mentioned both with a Warmth of regard he praised their uniform conduct & sensible of their attachment to his Person and Interest he had invested them with the most unlimited Powers to act as they should think proper.*[5]

According to Kuykendall, the relationship between the two former British sailors and Vancouver had historical significance.[6] Vancouver not only spoke in high praise of these two men, but he believed they could be of essential service in strengthening the alliance between Great Britain and Hawai'i. His confidence in them was not misplaced.

Like numerous other ship officers, Lieutenant Thomas Manby, in his journal of March 5, 1793, was impressed by the Hawaiians' view of Young and Davis. He noted that Kamehameha "has placed them and given them considerable authority in the Island; and their good conduct, I was happy to see, has gained them the confidence and good will of every inhabitant."[7]

James Macrae, in "With Lord Byron at the Sandwich Islands in 1825," wrote:

> *He [Byron] introduced me to Mr. Young. His name along with that of his companion, Mr. Davis, have long been distinguished in the history of these Islands. . . . the admission of the missionaries and their permanent residence, was [due to] the intercession of a few Englishmen, long residents on the islands, and without whose names any account of the first period of Hawaiian civilization would be imperfect. . . . That their names have not yet had any honorable mention in this connection . . . is one of the sins of omission which we would charitably overlook if we could. Those names were Young, Davis and Adams.*[8]

Captain Joseph Ingraham, of the brigantine *Hope,* appears to be the first American who records having met Young. He noted that "Young became the most important foreigner in the islands and the king's most trusted advisor."[9] "Mr. Young is respectable looking and appears a very sensible old man" was the opinion of Isaac Iselin, who also stated that "he promised to provide for all our work and arrangements made for our sick being lodged on shore in some of the king's habitations."[10]

A lengthier testimonial is given by Captain John Turnbull:

Mr. Young [is] a man of strict veracity. He has been long in the confidence of Tamehameha, whose fortunes he has constantly followed . . . and who gives him daily proofs of the sincerity of his attachment. He [Young] added that for several years Tamehameha had adopted it as a rule to request from all Europeans who touched within his dominions, a certificate or testimonial of his [Young's] good conduct towards them; but that now, considering his character for honesty and civility to be established, he no longer deems such certificates of any importance.[11]

Turnbull thought that Young, Davis, and James Stewart would have been assets in the district as magistrates or justices of the peace. "They would negotiate between the missionaries and natives, and being men of probity and character their good offices could not fail of having a desirable effect." Turnbull also recorded that "the first civilized methods of rule [in Hawai'i] emanated from the house of Young."[12] It was also noted that Young had been "given the rank of high chief, which placed him on a equal footing with the highest chiefs of the Hawaiian Kingdom."[13]

Annette Withington proclaimed:

There are no foreigners in the recorded history of Hawai'i who did more for the building up of the Hawaiian people than John Young, and Isaac Davis. . . . It seems remarkable that two sailors . . . were able to hold their own integrity, never departing from a strictly moral code in their own lives. They have been called the first missionaries. . . . With his keen insight Kamehameha must have soon recognized in these two sailors men whom he could trust.[14]

In a somewhat lighter vein, Alice Greenwell wrote that "John Young had a sense of humor which endeared him to the light-hearted Hawaiians."[15] Archibald Menzies, who visited the islands in 1793–94, observed:

John Young and Isaac Davis . . . made themselves extremely useful to us during the time we stayed, as they understood the manners and customs of the inhabitants and their language. One of them lived on each vessel, especially in the daytime, and transacted all business . . . and traffic between us and the natives, with such candor and fairness as entitles them to our approbation and regard and reflected much credit on their conduct.[16]

Some chroniclers later speculated that Young's adherence to Christian conduct may have derived from the early church association he had as a youth. Lucy Thurston, wife of pioneer missionary Asa Thurston, wrote in her autobiography: "He had long been a rare example in that degenerate age, of building a hedge about his family and standing in the gap thereof. . . . By marriage, by deeds and by counsel, the nation. Saxon blood flowed in his veins."[17]

An example of Young being his brother's keeper came about

when his old friend, Isaac Davis, died of being poisoned by jealous chieftains in 1810 . . . that he at once took the Davis children into his own [home] and brought them up with his own sons and daughters. His son James married a daughter of Davis and in his will Young equally divided his property with his own children and those of Isaac Davis.[18]

The historian John F. G. Stokes summed it up for many who knew of or about Young when he wrote: "John Young was a man of sterling worth." While Stokes's next statement does not relate to Young's character, he pointed out that "accounts by voyagers between 1790 and 1820 mention John Young more than anyone else except Kamehameha."[19]

Other than the observations of Young by secular visitors, the reflections by missionaries are far more favorable than they might have been for some wandering white foreigners. In March 1832 the veteran missionary Lorenzo Lyons and his wife were on their way to their assignment up in Waimea, probably having come from Kailua.

We reached Kawaihae about 5 PM. We took lodging in a native house with Mr. Young, an Englishman who was taken from an English ship [sic] about 45 years ago. He was made kind of a secretary to the king. . . . Mr. Young married a chiefess by whom he had several children. He is a righteous man, now 87 years old. His wife is a pious woman and a church member.[20]

The missionaries were always welcome at the Kawaihae home of the Youngs. Lyons, stationed at the Waimea mission, may have made visits more frequently than others, for he found the Young compound a convenient layover when he waited for a ship headed for Honolulu. Later, Lyons had his own dwelling on the Young property. Clarice Taylor, a Hawai'i newspaper feature writer, reports that Young was especially fond of Father Lyons and "spent hours with him arguing on the principles of religion in which they differed."[21]

In the same paper, prepared for the Daughters of Hawai'i, Taylor writes that John Young "was a deeply religious man . . . he brought up his children to be Christians and he practiced his faith."[22] Perhaps true, but lacking any evidence is Taylor's statement that Young trained as a layman in the Church of England.

Another reliable testimony to Young's Christian faith comes from the Reverend Artemis Bishop, who wrote that when he was about to leave the Young home for Kohala, he was persuaded by Young's wife, Kaoanaeha, to remain for the day "imparting religious instruction to herself and people." Bishop spent a whole morning answering questions and

giving advice in how they might best serve and worship God in their present condition, destitute of a spiritual guide. Mrs. Y. and several of her people have, for more than a year, been deeply interested in religious things . . . and feel the need of someone to lead them to the knowledge of God and salvation.

Bishop observed that the word of God "seems to have exerted a strong influence upon her, as well as upon some of her family." Prior to leaving for Kohala the next day at two o'clock in the morning (by canoe), Bishop recorded that he had "preached in the afternoon to a very attentive audience of about 150 people."[23] It was a good showing for Kawaihae.

Although as adults Young's two living sons had serious problems with alcohol, often while in government positions, there is no evidence that their father was ever anything but temperate in his drinking. In fact, when Kamehameha discovered the pleasures of demon rum, thanks to visiting ship captains, Young became quite concerned. Both Young and Davis may have been with the king when he had his first taste of liquor. According to Clarice Taylor, it was offered by Captain Maxwell and gladly accepted by Kamehameha at Kailua in 1791. The chiefs present were alarmed when they saw their leader under the influence. "They thought he had gone crazy and they wailed."[24] Young stepped in and was able to persuade the king to confine his indulgence to small quantities. It was said that eventually Kamehameha became a teetotaler, though he permitted the chiefs and his wives to drink of "the staggering water."[25] Mrs. Young (Kaoanaeha) did not drink, and as a churchgoer she taught her three daughters the evils of alcohol. They are said to have become teetotalers.

As for the pagan religion that surrounded him, Young was able not only to deal with it, but in one case he turned it to his advantage. A certain *kahuna,* like others in the king's chiefly circle, was jealous of Young and his favorable relations with the king. Kamehameha told Young that his (Young's) life was in danger because a certain *kahuna* was going to bring about his end by praying him to death. The *kahuna* had built a prayer hut in the woods to accomplish his deed. Young's reaction was not one of fear, but of retaliation. Two could play at that game, so within a few feet of the *kahuna*'s hut, Young built his own out of ti leaves. He let it be known that he would turn the tables, and he would pray his adversary to death. He positioned himself on his prayer mat and by whatever means he used, they played so deeply upon the superstitions of the *kahuna* "that he, in a short time, succumbed to the effect he desired accomplished upon Young." This turn of events made such an impression upon the natives "that no one tried their praying powers of him thereafter."[26]

Reference has been made to Young reading his Bible, one perhaps given him by Vancouver or another ship captain before the arrival of the missionaries. His journal, or "diary," made up, in general, of brief weather reports, contains a revealing piece of Young's religious bent. On one full page is what is believed to be the prayer poem of the early Saint Chrysostom. It is in handsome cursive handwriting, but whether it is Young's or copied by another is uncertain.

Withington speculates that while Young was not a missionary, "he nevertheless did some thinking about religion. His family background may have had a religious flavor since the parents named their three sons Peter, James and John."[27] Also among the forty-three pages of Young's journal is another poem with a spiritual focus. Whether it is Young's own creation or copied from another source cannot be determined, but it obviously appealed to Young, or he would not have taken the time and trouble to enter it. It reads, in part:

Life is the time to serve the Lord
The [time] to insure the great reward
And the lamp hold out to burn [that]
the vilest sinner may return.
Life is the hour that God has given
to escape from hell and fly to heaven.
The day of grace and mortals may
Secure the blessings of the day.
The living know that they must die.
But all the dead forget to lie
Their memory and their senses gone
Alike unknowing and unknown
Their hatred and their love is lost
Their envy buried in the dust
They have no share in all that is done
Beneath the circuit of the sun.

18 ❖ Evensong

When John Young suggested to Liholiho—Kamehameha II—and his chiefs that the missionaries be given a year's probation, it may well have been the last important advice he would give a sovereign, even though he was to live on under Kamehameha III for another fifteen years. Although Young is well remembered as a respected advisor to Kamehameha the Great in matters military as well as political and commercial, his counsel was seldom sought after 1820.

Historians are in agreement that Liholiho lacked the leadership skills of his father, not only his political and administrative acumen but also his athletic ability and military prowess. Whereas Kamehameha observed with vigor and force the *kapu* by which he lived and died, Liholiho soon abandoned them. In the final showdown Liholiho "wisely . . . called Kalanimoku and John Young for advice and counsel."[1] Young's involvement in modifying the *kapu* is described by Clarice Taylor: "At that important ceremony of free-eating, which the old system prohibited, John Young was given the duty of cutting up the food when Liholiho strode over to the women's table and ate with his mother."[2]

The young king and his court relocated from Kailua to Honolulu in about 1822. Young soon discovered that Ka'ahumanu, who proclaimed herself queen regent, had no need of an advisor such as himself, now enjoying well-earned tranquil retirement. Many of the king's counselors and *alii* had already passed on. Young had survived to become somewhat of an elder statesman. If his advice was seldom solicited by Liholiho, Young no doubt appreciated the freedom from kingly concerns.

Liholiho's reign was brief. In November 1823, with his half-sister–wife Kamāmalu, he departed on a trip to Great Britain, there to pay respects to King George IV, whose protection Liholiho believed Hawai'i enjoyed. In July of the following year both sovereigns died in London, felled by measles, a disease for which they had no immunity. The bodies of the royal couple were brought back to Hawai'i in a vessel commanded by Lord Anson Byron (cousin of the poet Lord George Gordon Byron). John

Young was then eighty years old and had no desire to be any sort of advisor to the late king's brother, who became Kamehameha III and would reign for thirty years.

The senior Young lived out most of the remaining thirteen years of his life at his Kawaihae homestead. As late as 1832 he was visited by the missionary Lorenzo Lyons. During the last decade of his life it can be deduced that he made more than one trip to Honolulu. There he stayed with his daughter Grace at the home of his son-in-law, Dr. Thomas Rooke.

From the accounts of travelers from 1816 on who visited Kawaihae, it is known that the *haole* chief was often referred to as "old John Young," an apt description, since he was then at least four score and more. He was one of the oldest residents in the Hawaiian Islands but in declining health.

James Macrae made such an observation in 1825: "Mr. Young has just come down from Owhyee. He is fast sinking under the infirmities of age."[3] Young lived for another decade. He was quite unafraid and well prepared to meet his maker. The missionary Sereno Bishop wrote of enjoying the Young family's hospitality in 1832. He also noted the beauty of the daughters, and observed at least one coffin suspended from the rafters. Apparently on more than one trip back from Honolulu Young brought with him a ready-made coffin. Ostensibly it was for himself or any other family member visited by the angel of death.[4]

The historian W. D. Alexander wrote a brief memorandum, now in the Hawaiian Historical Society archives, that "he [Young] came down from Kawaihae in very feeble health, and was under Dr. Rooke's care at Honolulu. He died December 16, 1835 at Rooke's place on Union St., and was buried at Puhukaina [*sic*] . . . mausoleum on King St."[5]

The journal of Stephen Reynolds adds but little more information on Young's final years. He wrote that on "Friday 7 October 1831 Mr. Young's family sailed for Hawai'i [Island]." This would be after a visit to the Rooke residence, in what is now in the heart of Honolulu's business district. Four years later, according to Reynolds, on August 13, 1835, Young was back in the city, probably for the last time. Wrote Reynolds: "Called to see Mr. Young" (date not given). On December 18 he entered in his journal, "John Young died at quarter past five. He had lived on the island [in the islands] about forty-three years." The following day, according to Reynolds, the "Chiefs [were] making preparation for the funeral of Mr. Young."[6]

The funeral was held December 18. Reynolds was more liberal with his information of the occasion:

Afternoon. The funeral of the late John Young, proceeded from Doct. Rooke's house to the native church [Kawaiaha'o]. Mr. [Bingham] made a prayer and a few remarks from the 90th Psalm. Mr. Tinker made last prayer. The corpse was then carried to the inclosure of the Cemetery of the Chiefs, where a grave had been prepared. . . . The Fort commenced firing Minute guns when the procession started. A certain number were fired from the Fort and on the Hill [Punchbowl] and the Shipping [presumably ships in Honolulu Harbor] followed. Ninety three guns were fired, one for each year of his age.[7]

Levi Chamberlain, one of the pioneer missionaries, wrote in a letter to G. P. Judd (dated December 20, 1835) that Young

was buried with military honors & his funeral was attended by a numerous concourse of people. The procession formed and proceeded to the meeting house where prayers were offered and an address in native and Eng. delivered by Mr. Bingham. The theme of the address was from the Ninetieth Ps. "The days of our years are three score and ten and if by reason of strength they be four score years yet it is their strength labor & sorrow. So teach us to number our days that we may apply our hearts to wisdom."[8]

Chamberlain concluded his letter by mentioning that Young had always been friendly to the missionaries, that his wife and one of his daughters were "members of the S. I. Church and two of his sons in law. His remains were deposited in the enclosure of the Royal Cemetery."[9] It was an appropriate

final resting place for the man who had so loyally served Hawaiʻi and who was part of the birth of the monarchy.

John Young had the great honor, as a high chief, of being laid to rest at Pohukaina, the mausoleum for Hawaiʻi's great, in what is now central Honolulu. He was the first non-Hawaiian to be so honored.[10] All of Hawaiʻi's early kings and chiefs were entombed there except for Kamehameha the Great ("Only the morning star knows . . .") and King Lunalilo, who is buried in a chapel with his father, Chief Charles Kanaʻina, on Kawaiahaʻo church grounds.

In 1863, twenty-eight years after Young's interment, the Royal Mausoleum was considered too crowded to accommodate any more remains. The Privy Council approved an idyllic location in Nuʻuanu Valley for those interred at Pohukaina and for future royal burials. In 1865 King Kamehameha V then arranged for the transfer of most caskets from Pohukaina to the new and final resting place. The ceremony involving the transfer was carried out in a way that the press of the day described as "a solemn scene."[11] The mile-and-a-half procession along King Street and up Nuʻuanu was at night.

Under the light of glaring torches and the full moon . . . King Kamehameha V [leading the procession] walked on foot accompanied by his venerable father [former governor Kekūanāoʻa] and most of the living chiefs. It was a sight worthy of a poet's pen, and one which may never again recur in the history of this people.[12]

Included in the lengthy procession were military companies (some of whom carried torches) and the cavalry. More significant was the presence of members of the royal family.

The torch-lit procession added to the solemnity of the occasion, and it was enhanced by both streets having been covered with *pili* grass to soften the sound of the horses' hooves and the wheels of the drays and carriages. The Hawaiian gods would approve such a ceremony.

For reasons unknown, only eighteen or twenty caskets were transferred at the time. John Young's was not among them, although other members of his family were. His was transferred the following year. It is a matter of record that in the intervening months Fanny, Emma's mother, wrote to Emma in London (in the Hawaiian language) of plans to transfer their father/grandfather. It was accomplished in late 1866, but no details are available as to what ceremony, if any, may have been observed. A special burial plot had been set aside and an appropriate marker provided later. John Young, the former Liverpool sailor, was laid to final rest in the pantheon of Hawai'i's great heros and high-born.

OPPOSITE: *The tomb of John Young at the Royal Mausoleum was reconstructed in 1997 to protect it from tree roots. The original tombstone was cleaned of its 165-year-old patina. The hour-long ceremony at its well-attended dedication included Hawaiian prayers and chants. Photograph courtesy Queen Emma Foundation*

The tombstone on Young's grave at the Royal Mausoleum reads: "Beneath this Stone are deposited the remains of JOHN YOUNG (of Lancashire in England) the Friend and Companion in Arms of KAMEHAMEHA who departed this life December 17th 1835, in the 93rd year of his age and the 46th of his residence on the SANDWICH ISLANDS." John Young was actually 91 years old when he died.

19 ❧ The Family

In that John Young had six children (two by his first wife and four by his second), it is surprising that the Young line has died out. By contrast Isaac Davis, who left only three children, has perhaps more than a hundred descendants in the islands, most on Hawai'i Island. Some are far removed, but with Davis blood nonetheless. The last of the Young descendants were two princes, and both were named Albert. The first was the only child of Emma and Kamehameha IV, and he died at the age of four. The second Albert was born to Lahilahi and Kamehameha III, and therefore he was a grandson of John Young and a great-grandson of Kamehameha the Great. He was Prince Albert Kūnuiākea who died an adult, without issue, in 1903. There are no known Young descendants, despite a wide search by the author that included inquiries in three Hawai'i newspapers for anyone claiming to be, or knowing of, a descendant of John Young.[1] (See Appendix IV.)

The first child of the Young family, Robert (his Hawaiian name is not known), was born February 14, 1796. He was sent to Boston by his parents at the age of six for an American education. This is attested to in a letter dated February 10, 1804, from Captain James Magee of the sailing vessel *Mandarin*. Written from Canton, it was addressed to "Mr. John Young Resident on the Sandwich Islands to the Care of Either Mr. Davis Capt Stewart or Mr Holms [*sic*]."[2] It reads:

I have sent you by Mr. Davis 20 pieces of Blue Nankeen and two boxes of tea. I left your son Robert in America about 6 months since, he is at school and behaves very well I shall do everything for him that I promis'd you may depend on it. I am very fond of him and shall take great care to make him a good man—Remember me to Stewart Davis & Holms when you see them & believe me your friend James Magee.

It is unknown whether Robert lived to adulthood, for in 1812, when he was sixteen, he joined the United States Navy. He was captured by the British in the battle of Lake Champlain and was sent as a prisoner of war to Bermuda, never to be heard of again. A search through naval records has failed to provide further information.

The second child and son, James Kānehoa, was born August 7, 1797, and he, too, was sent to Boston at an early age for his education. By his own admission, some years later, like his father, he forsook school at an early age for the life of a sailor. This gave him an opportunity to make several trips not only to America but also to England and, as did his father, to China. It was that experience as a seaman that gave him a proficiency in English, as did his Boston schooling, a gift that would serve him and his king well in later years.

After leaving the life of the sea Kānehoa became a close companion of Liholiho, and when that king and his wife, Kamāmalu, left on an official visit to Great Britain, Kānehoa accompanied the party as interpreter and translator.[3] Through a mishap in Rio de Janeiro, the letters of introduction to English royalty did not arrive on time. The mishap came about when Kānehoa had had too much to drink and missed his ship. According to Kamakau, he arrived in London on a coal ship with the letters.[4]

Kānehoa was also the bearer of official papers intended to convince the English monarch that his royal visitor was indeed the ruler of the Sandwich Islands.[5] It was then that the English king realized who his royal visitors were. In his capacity as interpreter, Kānehoa answered many questions that King George IV put to his visitor, though Liholiho and his consort had died of measles before the audience with King George could take place.

The bodies of the royal couple were sent back to Hawai'i in elaborate coffins on the British warship *Blonde*. Kānehoa returned on the same vessel, which made stops at Hilo and Maui before going to Honolulu with the royal remains.[6] Collins wrote that on the return trip from England, "Lord Byron placed the Hawaiians in the officers' gunroom. When his shocked officers refused to eat with the Hawaiians, Lord Byron told them they would either eat with their guests or in the forecastle with the sailors."[7]

Kānehoa Young was married three times, first to a daughter of Isaac Davis named Sarah. The ceremony was performed by an English chaplain, and Mrs. Judd states that it may have been the first Christian marriage in the Hawaiian Islands. They had no children. His second wife was named Ha'ale, by whom he had a daughter, Jane Lahilahi, named after his half-sister. His third wife, and widow at his death in 1851, was Hikoni, also called Kahele. Kānehoa adopted a male child named Keli'imaika'i (known as Alebada), the son of his half-sister Jane and Joshua Ka'eo.

When Kānehoa was governor of Maui he became greatly concerned over the high death rate of the Hawaiian people. He believed that intermarriage with Europeans was the only possible way of saving his people from extinction. He was also governor of Kaua'i for a short time.

At one point Kānehoa was, under King Kamehameha III, named as a member of the Board of Commissioners to Quiet Land Titles. He was also a member of the kingdom's House of Nobles. Shortly before his death, twenty-seven years after his visit to England, Kānehoa wrote a letter to W. C. Wyllie corroborating the fact that the royal visit was to establish Great Britain as a protectorate of the Sandwich Islands.[8] This was never carried out. That same year he fell victim to an epidemic and died at the age of fifty-four. Two weeks later his adopted son also died. Both are now interred in the Royal Mausoleum.

John Young's marriage to Kaoanaeha was in 1805. Their first child, born July 21, 1806, was a girl named Fanny Kakelaokalani (better known as Pane or Kekela). Fanny married a chief of the Moana line, George Nā'ea of Lahaina, but it was a union that failed to survive. Before its dissolution she gave birth to her only child, Emma Kaleleonālani, who would become the well-known Queen Emma, wife of Kamehameha IV. Fanny died in 1880 at the age of seventy-four, but lived long enough to see her daughter reign as queen and her father's remains interred among the great Hawai'ian *alii* in the Royal Mausoleum, where she too was buried.

The fourth of the Young children was Grace Kama'iku'i, born September 8, 1808. She was wedded to Dr. Thomas C. B. Rooke of Honolulu, physician to the royal court. The couple had no children of their own, but they adopted (*hanai*) Emma, daughter of Grace's sister Fanny.[9] Grace died in 1866 at the age of fifty-eight. She was the only Young to have married a *haole*.

John Young, Jr., better known as Keoni Ana, was born March 12, 1810, and like his other siblings was born at Kawaihae. He married a chiefess named Julia Alapa'i Kauwa. They had no children but *hanai* Peter Ka'eo, another son of Jane Lahilahi and Joshua Ka'eo. In 1845 Keoni Ana was named the monarchy's *kuhina nui*, or prime minister, under Kamehameha III and also Kamehameha IV. It was a position he held for nine years. A childhood friend of Kamehameha III, he served his king well. He was one of the chiefs who drew up the constitution of 1840, which transformed a feudal kingdom into a limited monarchy.

Before his death in 1857, he also served as governor of Maui, minister of the interior, chamberlain of the royal household, and a supreme court justice.[10] When Keoni Ana died in July 1857, he left much of his lands on the islands of Hawai'i, Moloka'i, Lāna'i, Maui, and O'ahu to his niece

Fanny Kakelaokalani Young Nāʻea,
John Young's daughter and mother
of Queen Emma.

Photograph. Bishop Museum, Honolulu

John Young, Jr., known as Keoni Ana,
c. 1850.

Photograph. Bishop Museum, Honolulu

Emma and his adopted sons, Peter Kaʻeo and Albert Kūnuiākea. Today a residential street in Waikiki carries the name Keoniana.

The last of John Young's family of six offspring was Jane Lahilahi ("the thin one"), born in May 1813. She was also called Gini or Kini. According to Clarice Taylor, she "was reared to be an intimate of Nāhiʻena-ʻena, the sacred daughter of Kamehameha."[11] Her husband was Joshua Kaʻeo, a scion of a Maui *alii*. The couple lived at court much of the time and eventually settled in Hale Kinau near Iolani Palace.[12] They had two sons. The first, Keliʻimaikaʻi (Alebada), was *hanai* to James Kānehoa Young, and the youngest, Peter (Kekuaokalani), was adopted by Keoni Ana.[13]

Chiefess Lahilahi was also mother to a son sired by King Kamehameha III. It was an arrangement agreed upon by both parties. On June 13, 1853, Prince Albert Kūnuiākea was born at Kuaihelani, later the site of the Central Union Church, which sat at the corner of Beretania and Richards Streets. "The last of the Kamehameha heirs to Hawaiʻi's throne," proclaimed the *Honolulu Advertiser* of March 11, 1903, when he died. It

The Family

also stated that this second Prince Albert was a grandson of Kamehameha the Great and was considered heir presumptive to the throne. The same source said he was brought up from infancy in the old Iolani Palace by Kamehameha III and his consort, Queen Kalama. He left a widow named Mary Poli, the widow of the Reverend Z. Poli, and no children. A mile-long procession of dignitaries and Roman Catholic societies bore the casket of the last known Young descendant from the palace to the Royal Mausoleum on Nuʻuanu Avenue.

From John Young's sizable family of five adults in Hawaiʻi, only three bore children: one by Kānehoa and his second wife Haʻale, one by Fanny, and three by Jane Lahilahi.

John Young may have been feeble in body in his declining years when, in 1834, he drew up his will (Appendix III), but he knew precisely how he wished to divide each of the thirty-eight parcels of extensive lands that were his. All of these lands had been given to him by King Kamehameha the Great, who had died fifteen years earlier.

To emphasize the good state of his mental health, he prefixed his wishes "Whereas, I, John Young, being of sound and perfect mind," then added parenthetically, "thanks be to God for the same." He followed by stating quite frankly that otherwise he was "of infirm health."

It was his first wish that "my dear wife Mary, otherwise called Kuamoo [Kaoanaeha], [be] in possession of all those lands which she antecedent [sic] to the date herself has received in free gift from me."[14] He then proceeded to identify those many lands and their locations. (See Appendix III.)

It was with clarity and generosity that he specified that in addition to the lands to be distributed among his own children, additonal lands were to be equally divided with "the surviving children of my departed friend, the late Isaac Davis, of Milford in England [Wales], in such manner as it may please His Majesty the King [Kamehameha III] and his Chiefs; Provided always that each and all of the said children receive a just and equal portion."[15] He continued: "Further, all the rest and residue of my estate, goods and chattels, I give and bequeath to be equally divided among my surviving children, such division to be superintended by His Brittanick Majesty's Consul, or such person or persons as he, the said Consul, may appoint."

He then named as his executors Captain Alexander Adams (the one-time husband of Sarah Davis, daughter of Isaac) and his own son-in-law, Dr. Rooke of Honolulu. On the back of the document was an endorsement, in

Hawaiian, signed by Kauikeaouli (King Kamehameha III). The will was witnessed by Dan T. Aborn and Charles Titcomb, and Kamehameha's signature was witnessed by Richard Charlton, his British majesty's "Consul for the Sandwich, Society and Friendly Islands." (That was a geographic spread of a couple of thousand miles for Consul Charlton.)

It would not be until after the Great Mahele—the dividing of all lands—of 1848 that some of the lands were to become the properties of Young and Davis survivors.[16] After Young's death his children had, as a family unit, agreed upon which lands should go to whom. There were thirty-eight different parcels listed, totaling several thousand acres, and on four islands. The names of the lands, their location, and the various recipients follow.[17]

Hālawa, ʻEwa, Oʻahu:	1/2 Grace Kamaʻikuʻi Rooke
Halea [Haleu], Maui:	Fanny (Pane) Kakelaokalani
Halekēhaku, Hāmākualoa, Maui:	Keoni Ana (John Jr.)
Hianaoli, Kona:	Betty (Peke) Davis
Honokahua, Kāʻanapali, Maui:	Sarah (Kale) Davis
Hoomaliohalaoa [Hālawa], Hawaiʻi:	Kaoanaeha (Mary)
Kahului, Kona:	Grace Kamaʻikuʻi Rooke
Kailua, 2 small *ili*, Kona	
Kalama, Kona:	Grace Kamaʻikuʻi Rooke
Kamoamoa, Puna:	Kaoanaeha (Mary)
Kaʻōpapa, Kona	
Kapaʻa, Kohala:	Sarah (Kale) Davis
Kapaloakua, Lahaina	
Kaupō, Kohala:	Kaoanaeha (Mary)
Kawaihae (East), Hawaiʻi:	Keoni Ana (John Jr.)
Kealahewa, Hawaiʻi:	Kaoanaeha (Mary)
Kapewakua, Maui:	Betty (Peke) Davis
Kiʻilae, Kona:	George Hūʻeu Davis
Kiʻiokalani, Hawaiʻi:	Fanny (Pane) Kakelaokalani
Koloakiu:	Kaoanaeha (Mary)
Kukuwau (Kukuua-iki), Hilo:	George Hūʻeu Davis
Kukuwau (Kukuau-nui), Hilo:	Keoni Ana (John Jr.)
Kukuihala, Puna:	Kaoanaeha (Mary) (King's Mahele 258)
Kūpeke, Molokaʻi:	Betty (Peke) Davis
Maunalei, Lānaʻi:	Fanny (Pane) Kakelaokalani
Opuowao [Opuoao], Kohala:	Kaoanaeha (Mary)

ʻŌuli, Kohala	
Pāhoa, Kona	
Pāhoa, Waikiki, Oʻahu:	Keoni Ana (John Jr.)
Pāhoehoe-iki, Kona:	Fanny (Pane) Kakelaokalani
Pāhoehoe-nui, Kona:	Jane (Gini) Lahilahi
ʻUlaʻino, Hāna, Maui:	James Kānehoa
Waiaka-iki, Kohala:	Jane (Gini) Lahilahi
Waiaka-nui, Kohala:	Jane (Gini) Lahilahi
Waikā, Kohala:	Jane (Gini) Lahilahi
Waikahekahe-iki, Puna:	Sarah (Kale) Davis
Waikahekahe-nui, Puna:	Jane (Gini) Lahilahi
Waikoloa, Hawaiʻi:	George Hūʻeu Davis

According to Stokes, "the lands would be worth millions of dollars today."[18] That was his opinion in 1932. Today many of the lands of John Young are worth ten times Stokes's estimate. One of the largest beneficiaries is today's Queen Emma Foundation. It came into ownership of several thousand acres, largely the *ahupuaʻa* that had been given John Young by Kamehameha. The property came to the Foundation by virtue of Fanny's inheritance, which she left to her daughter, Queen Emma. Also, Emma's adoptive mother, Grace Young Rooke, passed on her share to Emma. She in turn willed most of it to Queen's Hospital, now under the umbrella of the Queen Emma Foundation.

20 ✤ Queen Emma

Her Kawaihae beginnings were humble enough. The native house in which she was born had no fancy trappings. Beyond that, she was the only child of Fanny Kakelaokalani Young and chief George Nāʻea of Lahaina. Despite the early separation of her parents (Fanny never remarried) and her remote and modest birthplace, she was to become every inch a queen, and a much-beloved one at that.

Emma was born January 2, 1836, only two weeks after the death of her grandfather, John Young. She was of royal blood by virtue of her grandmother, Kaoanaeha, and thus the great-granddaughter of Keliʻimaikaʻi, the full brother of Kamehameha the Great. Her birth name was Kalanikaumakeamano. After the death of her son and then her husband, she took the name Kaleleonālani, meaning "the flight of the heavenly chiefs."[1]

As a young child she was adopted by Dr. Rooke and his wife, Grace, of Honolulu. The couple was childless, and since it was often the custom to

The grass shack at Kawaihae said to be the 1836 birthplace of Queen Emma.
Photograph by Brigham. Bishop Museum, Honolulu

allow close friends or relatives to *hanai* a child, the baby was promised to Grace and her husband before the birth. It was a fortunate setting for the girl, being reared in a home where British manners and culture were the norm. Her urban life was enhanced by attendance for a time at the Chiefs' Children's School. There she was in the company of other high-born children, and it was there that she met young Alexander Liholiho, whom she would marry when he was King Kamehameha IV. When she no longer attended the royal school, she had the advantage of an English governess. The combination, and the environment, gave her a well-rounded education and some immersion in Western ways.

It also introduced her to royal ways, for on June 19, 1856, when she was twenty years old, after a respectable engagement, she was married to Alexander Liholiho, who reigned as Kamehameha IV. By then he had been Hawaiʻi's king for two years, succeeding his adoptive father, Kamehameha III. Her new husband also had royal blood, being the grandson of Kamehameha the Great. Not only had he attended the royal school, but as a youth he had traveled with his older brother, Lot, under the guidance of Dr. G. P. Judd, to Europe and some American cities. (In New York City he had been ordered out of a railway car because of the color of his skin. The incident caused him to shun America and its culture in favor of British connections and behavior. Indeed, the royal couple shared strong inclinations toward a British way of life.)

The wedding was royal in every sense of the word. The ceremony was held at the venerable Kawaiahaʻo church, Hawaiʻi's Westminster Abbey. The bride was given away by her foster father (her biological father, George Nāʻea, had died two years earlier). The couple was united according to the Anglican rite. All in all, including the reception held at the royal palace, it was a glittering affair—the social event for many a season to come.

The king looked splendid in his royal regalia, while the bride, who with her attendants arrived in a flower-trimmed carriage, was dressed in a shimmering white silk gown. After the ceremony a lei-decked carriage drove them to the palace. The streets were lined with admirers, many of whom lay prostate before the king, as their fathers had done before their king. The carriage traveled over streets covered with rush, which deadened the sound of the carriage wheels.[2]

The wedding gifts were lavish. Green cut glass and a set of Copeland china came from Victoria, Queen of the British Empire. A complete silver service was sent by Napoleon III. That same French ruler later sent a pair of silver candelabra, a unique clock, and a stereopticon that was one of its kind and is on display at the Queen Emma Summer Palace.

Two years later, on May 20, 1858, a twenty-one-gun salute from the battery of a cannon on Punchbowl Hill heralded the birth of their only child, a son. It was cause for a "joyous event for the royal pair, who held court in European style."[3] This was the first royal birth since the days of

Queen Emma, John Young's granddaughter, reigned with King Kamehameha IV (Alexander Liholiho) and remained active for years after his early death.
Hawai'i State Archives

Alexander Liholiho, who became King Kamehameha IV, married his childhood sweetheart, Emma Kaleleonālani Nā'ea (Rooke), in June 1856.
Hawai'i State Archives

Kamehameha I. (It would also be the last child born to reigning Hawaiian monarchs for the remaining forty years of the kingdom.) They named him Albert, for the consort of Queen Victoria. Hawai'i's Privy Council bestowed upon him the title of His Royal Highness, the Prince of Hawai'i, and recognized him as the heir-apparent to the throne. He was christened with the ritual of the Church of England. Queen Victoria agreed to be godmother-by-proxy to the prince, and she dispatched a huge silver cup commemorating Albert's birth and baptism.

Just as Emma's appreciation of the Anglican religion and her British inclinations stemmed from her foster father, so did her interest in establishing a hospital in the city. The royal couple was aware of the alarming death rate from imported diseases. Half a century earlier the population of the kingdom was over two-hundred-fifty thousand. Now it had dwindled to only

"The Prince of Hawai'i," the only child and heir of Queen Emma and King Kamehameha, in a painting made about the time of his death in 1862 at the age of four. Named after Prince Albert, consort of Queen Victoria of Great Britain, he had been Hawai'i's hope for continuing the Kamehameha dynasty.

Painting by Enoch Wood Perry.

Bishop Museum, Honolulu

seventy-five thousand, and of those, ten thousand lived in the growing city of Honolulu. Dr. Rooke had his dispensary in his home. He was also the royal commissioner of public health and the court physician. None of this was lost on the queen, who with her husband's full support, pressed for a hospital. The king, who had always been concerned about his subjects' health, helped in the fund-raising by going hat-in-hand among the offices and shops in the city. Between them, the royal couple raised thousands of dollars. So appreciative of his wife's input and tireless efforts was the king that he named the new medical center the Queen's Hospital. Today Queen's Medical Center has expanded over a full city block and is among the finest and most up-to-date health centers in the Pacific Rim.

Emma and her husband are also credited with the introduction of the Anglican church to Hawai'i. It was Lady Jane Franklin, wife of Sir John Franklin, the famed arctic explorer, who happened to be in Honolulu, and who convinced Emma to write Queen Victoria and ask that an Anglican bishop be sent to Hawai'i. Queen Emma did, and Queen Victoria did, and a bishop arrived in Honolulu soon after. Queen Emma also solicited and raised funds for a school for girls, now known as St. Andrew's Priory. Today a main thoroughfare, Queen Emma Street, borders both the Anglican cathedral and the priory.

The Queen's Hospital, founded by Queen Emma in 1859 with the help of her royal husband, Kamehameha IV, was Honolulu's first modern hospital. Today it sprawls over a large city block and is known as Queen's Medical Center.
Photograph. Hawaiian Historical Society, Honolulu

In 1862 joy turned to ashes with the sudden death of the young prince. The king tried to busy himself by translating into his native tongue the Anglican Book of Common Prayer, but the angel of death lingered on. Fifteen months after the death of his son and heir, Kamehameha IV, aggravated by severe asthma, remorseful over an earlier scandal, and grieving for the loss of his son, died. He was succeeded on the throne by his older brother Lot, Kamehameha V, the last of the Kamehamehas to reign.

The death of her only child and then her husband, all within a span of fifteen months, left a stricken queen. The story is told that after her husband's death, in her grief Emma chose to live in the west wing of the chapel on the grounds of the Royal Mausoleum. Servants saw that she had food and a place to sleep. In that way she felt she would be close to her only child and her husband.[4] After a month (Queen Liliuokalani surmised it may have been two weeks) she was persuaded to end her vigil and return to her home and friends.

It was after her husband's death that Emma decided to take a trip abroad. Through prior correspondence she had become a friend of Queen Victoria, whom she planned to visit. While in England, Emma made it a point to raise funds for the construction of what would later become St. Andrew's Cathedral, as well as for the completion of the Episcopal (Anglican) school for girls, St. Andrew's Priory. She spent six months in England, and before she left was entertained by Queen Victoria at Windsor Castle. (Their correspondence would continue.) Later Emma and her retinue visited the Continent where she was warmly welcomed by nobility. On her return to Hawai'i she visited Washington, D.C., where she was graciously received by President Andrew Johnson.[5]

In 1874 Emma found herself once again part of the political swirl in the kingdom of Hawai'i. Her husband had died without naming a successor. Alexander's brother Lot, who succeeded him as Kamehameha V, reigned for nine years. But the bachelor king also died without naming a successor. So did his successor, King Lunalilo, and, according to the constitution, this called for an election by the Legislative Assembly. Emma, the queen dowager, was persuaded to be a candidate. Her opponent was David Kalākaua, a popular figure, the postmaster general who had a substantial following. The contest was long, drawn out, and very acrimonious. Kalākaua, a seasoned campaigner, was supported by the American business interests, while Emma was criticized for being too pro-British. Kalākaua won a substantial victory, but there was a bitter ending to the contest. Many of the dowager's faithful friends took to the streets and attacked the main courthouse, causing considerable damage. Things simmered down only after marines from visiting warships were called to intervene. On February 13, 1874, Emma acknowledged Kalākaua as the king of the Hawaiian Islands, and she asked her followers to do the same.

Many of Emma's last years were spent at her Nu'uanu Valley residence, now the setting for the beautiful Queen Emma Summer Palace, an attractive and charming museum under the auspices of the Daughters of Hawai'i. The sizable piece of property in Nu'uanu Valley is approximately where, in 1795, Emma's grandfather, John Young, along with Isaac Davis and King Kamehameha, held council as O'ahu's final and bitter battle was being waged.

In the mid-1800s this large one-story home was the property of John Young, Jr. (Keoni Ana). He called it Hānaiakamālama, after a favorite spot in Kawaihae. The name means "foster child of the god Kalama," Kalama being one of the gods who supposedly watched over the Young family. It was appropriate that Emma, born with Young family blood and royal blood, kept the name, by which the edifice is still known.[6]

Emma's last years were spent in the company of close friends and in letter writing. She kept up a correspondence with Queen Victoria, who would outlive her by sixteen years. Emma was a prodigious letter writer. The Queen Emma file in the Hawai'i State Archives includes close to two thousand letters and notes either from or to Emma. About one hundred twenty-five of them represent correspondence between Emma and her cousin, Peter Ka'eo, during his few years at the Hansen's disease settlement at Kalaupapa.

Emma's well-rounded education and her culture are reflected in verses she wrote after Alexander Liholiho's death. "Some of her most poignant work was shown in the poetry composed after the death of her son and her husband."[7] They are long and moving lamentations in her Hawaiian tongue, and they mirror her rich native heritage. Despite her apparent enjoyment in writing, she could not be persuaded to put her memoirs into writing, feeling that she was not competent, though she had contributed to Hawai'i's history during her lifetime.

Her last years were spent at Rooke House, on the *makai*-Waikiki corner of Beretania and Nu'uanu Streets, which her foster father, who died in 1858, left to her. Also living with her there, and sometimes at the summer palace, which Emma often retreated to, was her birth mother, Fanny Young Nā'ea. Emma, always religious, became even closer to her faith and continued to support the growing Episcopal church. Far from being a recluse, she entertained occasionally and enjoyed social visits with her contemporaries. In her final year she suffered a few strokes, the last one being fatal.

John Young's only granddaughter died in 1885 at the age of forty-nine. She is buried at the Royal Mausoleum, only a mile from her beloved summer palace, next to her husband and the royal prince of Hawai'i. There she also joined a number of other Youngs, beginning with her grandfather, who were privileged to rest among the *alii*. Emma is still regarded as a beloved queen. She demonstrated her love for her people by her ardent crusade for the hospital. Her personal achievement was to see the entry of the Anglican church (first designated "the Reformed Catholic Church") into Hawai'i. To the end she remained opposed to annexation and considered herself better protected by the British lion than the American eagle.

She was generous in her will, which was drawn up at Rooke House a few months before her death. To her various servants she left what would then be substantial monetary gifts. To some friends she left specific pieces of property, mostly located in the city. There were several thousand acres of land to be disposed of, mostly on Oʻahu and Hawaiʻi Island. These were lands she had inherited from her adoptive mother, Grace Young Rooke; from her real mother, Fanny Young Nāʻea; and from an uncle, Bennett Namakeha. The principal beneficiaries were (and are to this day) the then-called Queen's Hospital, and to a lesser degree, St. Andrew's Priory. The *ahupuaʻa* of Kawaihae, given to her grandfather by Hawaiʻi's first king, is among the lands to which today's Queen Emma Foundation has title.

Queen Emma's epitaph could well be that she was a woman of a kind and lovable nature who brought to the palace a high degree of refinement and culture.

21 ❧ Will the Real John Young Please Stand Up?

About fifteen years after John Young's death in 1835, there surfaced in New England two separate families, one from Massachusetts and the other from Connecticut, who declared John Young to be an ancestor. The first mention of this, from Massachusetts in 1850, is suspiciously close to the 1848 Great Mahele when the vast land holdings of John Young would have become public information. However, there appears to be no evidence that the New England families made any property claims. That might have come later had their assertions not been scotched by well-informed Hawai'i sources.[1]

Letters from New Englander Otis Young from 1932 to 1934 are on file with the Hawaiian Historical Society, the Bishop Museum, the Hawai'i State Archives, and the Hawaiian Mission Children's Society, in which, the historian Stokes says, the writer was "arguing the matter with the librarians." Pertinent information from Hawai'i publications and manuscripts were forwarded, "copies of which are available in New England libraries; yet the various members of the families concerned appear to be unaware of it."

In 1913, Honolulu's Episcopal bishop, Henry Restarick, later the president of the Hawaiian Historical Society, was in Boston and had the opportunity to examine the material and documents of the Massachusetts family. It was their contention that Hawai'i's John Young was born at Wellfleet, on Cape Cod, February 2, 1759, to John and Rebecca Young. He was known as David but, for reasons not given, later took the name of John, thus muddying the waters. (His birth date is fifteen years later than John Young of Hawai'i.) The Massachusetts documents also make a strong case for their man having been on Metcalfe's *Eleanora* and detained on Hawai'i. But their case gets wobbly when they say he had to hide in a hogshead, was rescued by a beautiful Hawaiian princess (presumably Kaoanaeha), whom he of course married. Some of their children did carry the same first names of the Hawai'i Young family. There were indeed similarities, but much of their information was second or third hand, and hearsay. So convinced was Restarick of the likelihood that John Young had been a native of Massachusetts, that he wrote a detailed article for the 1913 annual report of the Hawaiian Historical Society. It was titled "John Young of Hawai'i, an American."

John Young, by Jacques Etienne Arago.
Lithograph. Bishop Museum, Honolulu

John Young, by D. Pellion.
Lithograph. Bishop Museum, Honolulu

For a long time it has been thought that there was only one extant illustration of John Young, and it was by Jacques Etienne Arago, a draftsman under Captain Louis de Freycinet when the French corvette Uranie was briefly anchored in Kawaihae Bay in 1819. As it happened, another artist aboard the Uranie was D. Pellion and he too executed an image of Young at approximately the same time. John Young was then seventy-five years of age and it shows in Pellion's work.

De Freycinet himself noted in his journal that he found Young ill and aging, still mourning the loss of King Kamehameha a few months earlier. While Pellion's work depicts an old John Young, Arago has his subject as middle-aged at best. There are two or three possibilities for such a difference in Arago's sketch: he may have made the decision to sketch Young as middle-aged; markings on the lithograph indicate that the image was drawn by L. Lobin after Arago's sketch, and he may have taken the liberty of portraying a much younger subject; if neither of these two altered Young's features, it could have been done by the hands of the lithographer, a man named Villain.

Arago's illustration appeared in his book Voyage autour du monde (Paris: Horter and Ozaane, 1839), vol. 3, facing p. 181.

The Connecticut claimants asserted that the right John Young was born in 1763 (nineteen years after Hawai'i's John Young) in Windham County, to John and Zerviah Huntington Young. Like earlier claims, they are based on family tradition, much of it not written down until years later. Some of their records make much of five points, the first being that they, too, "had a son who wrote a sketch of his line of the Youngs in 1850." Restarick mistakenly wrote that David changed his name to John. This John, like others, married in Hawai'i and had sons influential in local politics. This last statement fits. But that evidence is nullified by another statement that son John did not marry, but instead "was massacred in the Sandwich Islands." This is a matter of being confused with the *Fair American*. Another claim is made that he was a privateer in the American Revolution, taken prisoner, then after his release shipped on board the *Eleanora*, "whose crew was massacred at the Sandwich Islands, and he among them, unmarried."

Other Connecticut assertions are that "David . . . was a sea captain, possibly of a privateer, was sent to the Sandwich Islands as a prisoner and died there at age of 72."

There is no doubt that both New England families had well-preserved family records and fairly well-prepared family genealogies. John Young of Lancashire, born much earlier than any of the later John (or David) Youngs, had nothing to show in the way of birth records. In England of 1744, such registrations were nonexistent or not implemented. As for records that Young may have had relating to his nativity, Stokes says: "His personal papers were destroyed by a flood 40 years ago." That would have been 1898.[2]

What we do know of Young's nativity and earlier life comes from U.S. Commissioner David Gregg's letter, in which he specifically states that Young was born in Great Crosby, Lancashire, March 17, 1744, to Robert and Grace Young. Gregg states that he was given that information by Dr. Rooke, who obviously got it from his son-in-law.

What does exist in support of John Young of Hawai'i being British are the written records of nearly fifty visitors, especially sea captains or Young's contemporaries. Thirty-six of these individuals provide information, though it is indirect, testifying to Young's English origins. The amount is considerable and it is consistent. Probably the earliest is from the aforementioned American ship captain, Joseph Ingraham, commander of the brigantine *Hope*. He identified "Jno. Young" as "an English man born." Others who knew him described him as either English or British.

The clincher may well be Captain Vancouver's offer to Young and Davis of free passage back to their homeland. He had also recorded "John Young, an English seaman" and again "John Young, born at Liverpool." But nothing would be more convincing than his identifying "our two countrymen, Young and Davis."[3]

A complete end to the subject may be Bishop Restarick's about face in 1924, eleven years after his article supporting those somewhat convincing American claims. After closer examination, he backed away from his support of Massachusetts claims, citing that the facts undermined his previous position.[4] The long and short of it all is that John Young is a common name, that many men with that name became American sailors, that there were at least three other men named John Young in the Hawaiian Islands at about the same time, and early Honolulu directories list a great number of them.

Epilogue ❁ The Old Homestead

Since 1973 the John Young homestead at Kawaihae, along with the nearby Puʻukoholā Heiau, has been under the jurisdiction of the National Park Service, the property having been donated by the Queen Emma Foundation. The entire Young compound is about two acres. It had been entirely neglected until the Hawaiʻi National Park Service took over in recent years. One of the first concerns of the Park Service was the stabilization of the main western structure. Excavation of one structure was completed in 1978.

The Park Service took on the project in part because Young was recognized as a person of importance and influence in the service of Kamehameha the Great. Either directly or indirectly, he was part of the picture that formed the early post-contact Hawaiian Islands. The study was also considered highly important for the linkages it might provide in regards to customs and cultures of that early nineteenth-century period. It was especially significant in view of Young's home being the first Western-style domicile in the Islands.[1]

Under the supervision of project archaeologist Paul Rosendahl, the crew of five commenced excavations in mid-July 1978 and continued for the next two months. It was assumed, correctly, that the field work and findings would give insight to living conditions of over 175 years ago, reflecting both Western and Hawaiian cultures.

After surface rubble and dirt had been removed, the fruit of the workers' labors became evident. Over one thousand "portable items" were salvaged and identified, and they included traditional Hawaiian objects as well as Western. All represented about a half century (1793–1840) of living in one location. In addition to mammal bones and shells were such revealing objects as brass buttons; beads; gun parts; nails; 180 other iron objects; a chimney glass; gun flints; a writing slate; a stone anvil; ceramics, including porcelain sherds and Canton ware; one complete bottle; and numerous pieces of copper, bronze, and wire fragments. Tools that came to light were files, abraders, a hammer stone, an awl, and brass needles. Unexpected was the discovery of a small crypt that contained the remains of an infant and a small child. All told, these diversified items reflected an environment and a slice of life in the Young household that were not apparent in the surviving pages of Young's journal.

Today the homestead of John Young is less than a skeleton of its former self. Abandoned about 1850, shortly after Kaoanaeha died (and then long neglected), its various units are indiscernible, except for the main dwelling. It has four partially remaining walls with interior plastering and a temporary metal shelter over existing walls put in place to preserve the structure. Gone too is the upper loft, recorded by Laura Judd. Elsewhere on the ground are vague man-made rock lines that formed "platforms" or floors and foundations for other structures. Erosion has taken its toll.

Several years ago, when Alfred P. Taylor was the librarian for the Hawai'i State Archives, he felt that the remaining structure should be restored and preserved. He pointed out that "it was there that all ship captains and many others generally consulted with John Young before having an audience with Kamehameha, and . . . it was there that much of the governmental foundation for the new Kingdom of Hawai'i was studied out."[2] The suggestion was pleasing to Governor Lawrence Judd, who envisioned plans for a "John Young Park." Nothing came of the proposal then or later. There have been similar proposals made by concerned citizens, but not at a high level of government. An inquiry in 1997 to Bryan Harry, superintendent for the Pacific Island System, Support Office Service of the National Park Service, regarding its interest in restoring the Young dwelling and possibly following up on Governor Judd's plan for a park, produced the reply that "we have not decided to do that at this time."

It was fortunate indeed that the National Park Service archaeological project took place when it did, for thirteen years later, in July 1991, a raging brush fire swept the lands of the John Young homestead. In an attempt to control the conflagration, a bulldozer was brought in by the county to clear the brush around the homesite. It was like the proverbial bull in a china shop. The treads of the metal monster crushed, among other things, the stone walls that were the homesite's perimeter. Foundations of stone platforms for former units were flattened. The damage was considerable. In early 1992 a team of Park Service field workers under the supervision of Laura Carter Schuster worked to survey and estimate the damage. Park Service staff constructed a cable fence with steel posts to identify the land as part of Pu'ukoholā. The site has remained the same since.

The partially restored John Young residence at Kawaihae.
Photograph. Courtesy National Park Service

There has been public interest in restoring the Young homestead, if not to its former glory with all five or six units, at least the main dwelling. Funding from the National Park Service Cultural Resource Preservation Program was secured in 1997 to complete reassessment of existing stabilization and determine future interpretive potential. More recently, funding has been secured for a joint project between the National Park Service and the University of Hawaii–Hilo to provide for further excavations and the stabilization of existing walls.

Appendices

Appendix I
Louis Choris's Account of John Young's Life

Louis Choris was the artist on the Russian ship Rurick *when it visited Hawai'i in 1817. He gave an account of John Young's life in his* Voyage pittoresque autour du monde, *pp. 7–9 (translated from the French). His story is as he probably heard it from Young.*

John Young, who is known by descriptions by travelers who preceded us to this archipelago, where he has lived for twenty-six (26) years, came to meet us. He is loved and esteemed by the King and his people. He is 83 years old. When we arrived there in 1817 he was very weak, in such a manner that there was little hope that he would survive much longer.[1] He was the supervisor [boatswain or bosun] of the crew of an American ship which arrived in March 1790 at Ovaihy [Hawai'i]. On the 17th Young obtained permission to stay on land until the next day; but when he tried to return to the ship he found all the pirogues [canoes] taboo and beached on the shore, and Kamehameha declared that if he tried to use a native boat he would be put to death, but one would be furnished to him the next day. However, knowing that a schooner commanded by the son of the American captain, had been apprehended in a bay south [*sic*] of Ovaihy, and that [undecipherable] four of the five men who manned the ship had been killed by the natives, the king would not permit Young to leave; he treated him with great friendship.

Young's ship which had left the anchorage to take advantage of a favorable wind, stopped for two days in front of Kealakekua Bay, firing cannon volleys to alert Young, and approaching the coast whenever it was possible; finally a change of wind forced them to [lift anchor and sail away].[2]

When Young realized that he was forced to stay and live in a country where he was ignorant of the language, where there were no other Europeans, and from which he could not escape soon other than by an extraordinary event, he was crestfallen. The king sought to console him and give him courage; he held him in such affection and esteem, gave him fields and men to cultivate them, also presented him with pigs as a gift, and finally ordered his chiefs to treat him with friendship and respect.

With this start, he became one of the richest landowners. He learned the language, married a woman of distinguished class, and was elevated to the rank of a chief; he decided to end his days on the island. Before he reached his rank [?] he formed a plan with another Englishman [Isaac Davis] to escape but this failed.

After that time he was resigned to his fate; his good conduct with the natives and the foreigners who came to this island, gained him overall esteem and the unlimited confidence of Kamehameha. All his [the king's] affairs passed through his [Young's] hands.

Appendix II
"John Young" Letter

This letter, signed by John Young and dated November 27, 1826, was probably written by Hiram Bingham or one of his colleagues.

Kawaihae, Island of Hawaii, Nov. 27, 1826

Whereas it has been represented by many persons that the labors of the missionaries in these islands are attended with evil and disadvantage to the people, I hereby most cheerfully give my testimony to the contrary. I am convinced that the good which it is accomplishing and already effected, is not little. The great and radical change already made for the better, in the manners and customs of this people, has far surpassed my most sanguine expectations. During the forty years that I have resided here, I have known thousands of defenceless human beings being cruelly massacred in their exterminating wars. I have seen multitudes of my fellow beings offered in sacrifice to their idol gods. I have seen this large island, once filled with inhabitants, dwindle down to its present few in numbers through wars and disease, and I am persuaded that nothing but Christianity can preserve them from total extinction. I rejoice that true religion is taking place of superstition and idolatry; that good morals are superseding the reign of crime; and that a code of Christian laws is about to take the place of tyranny and oppression. These things are what I have longed for, but have never seen till now. I thank God that in my old age I see them, and humbly trust I feel them too.

John Young

Appendix III
Last Will and Testament of John Young

Reprinted from Thomas Thrum, Hawaiian Annual, *1911, pp. 102ff.*

In the name of God, Amen! Whereas, I, John Young, being of sound and perfect mind, thanks be to God for the same, but of infirm health, do make and ordain this my last Will and Testament in manner and form following, namely:

First, I hereby bequeath and confirm my dear wife Mary, otherwise called Kuamoo, in possession of all those lands which she antecedent to the date herself has received in free gift from me, To Wit:

One land situated in the District of Puna and called Kamoamoa; also one land situated in the District of Hamakua and called Koloakiu; also four lands in the District of Kohala, namely: Opuowao, Hoomaliohalaoa, Kealahewa, and Kaupo, all on the Island of Hawaii: further, all the rest and residue of the lands which I hold possession of under the King and Chiefs of the Sandwich Islands, To Wit:

Twenty-three lands on the Island of Hawaii, namely; Kukuihala, Waika-hekahe-nui, Waikahekahe-iki, in the District of Puna; Kukuwau-nui and Kukuwau-iki, in the District of Hilo; Waikoloa, Waiaka-nui, Waiaka-iki, Ouli, Kapaa, Waika, Kuokalani and Kawaihae in the District of Kohala; Hianaloli, Kahului, Pahoehoe-nui, Pahoehoe-iki, Pahoa, Kaopapa, Kalama, Kiilae, and two small Iiis at Kailua, in the District of Kona.

Five lands on the Island of Maui, namely: Ulaino in the District of Hana, Halehaku in the District of Hamakualoa, Honokahua in the District of Kaanapali, Kapaloa and Halea in the District of Lahaina. One land on the Island of Molokai called Kupeke, and two lands on the Island of Oahu, namely: Halawa in District of Ewa, and Pahoa in the District of Waikiki.

I give and bequeath to be equally divided between my surviving children and the surviving children of my departed friend, the late Isaac Davis, of Milford in England, in such manner as it may please His Majesty the King and his Chiefs; Provided always that each and all of the said children receive a just and equal portion. Further, all the rest and residue of my estate, goods and chattels, I give and bequeath to be equally divided among my surviving children, such division to be superintended by His Brittanick Majesty's Consul, or such person or persons as he, the said Consul, may appoint.

Further, I nominate, constitute and appoint Alexander Adams and Thomas Charles Byde Rooke Joint Executors of this my last Will and Testament, hereby Revoking all other and former Wills by me at any time heretofore made.

In witness whereof, I have hereunto set my hand and seal this twenty-six day of June in the year of Our Lord One thousand eight hundred and thirty-four.

[Signed] John Young [seal]

Witnessed (in due form) by
Dan T. Aborn
Chas. Titcomb

Appendix IV
John Young Family Tree

For more detailed information on John Young's family, see chapter 19
("The Family"). The following begins with Young's parents, the first known
generation in Lancashire, c.1740.

(1) Robert Young m. Grace (maiden name unknown)
    (2) Peter Young
    (2) James Young
    (2) John Young m. Namokuelua (there is no evidence of other siblings
        of Peter, James, or John)
        (3) Robert Young
        (3) James Kānehoa Young m. Sarah (Kale) Davis (no issue)
        (3) James Kānehoa Young m. Haʻale (second marriage)
            (4) Jane Lahilahi Young m. Nuʻuanu
                (5) Samuel Nuʻuanu
        (3) James Kānehoa Young m. Hikoni (Kahele) (third marriage; no issue)
    (2) John Young m. Kaoanaeha (Mary) (second marriage)
        (3) Fanny (Pane) Kakelaokalani Young m. George Nāʻea
            (4) Emma Kaleleonālani Nāʻea (Rooke) m. Alexander Liholiho
                (King Kamehameha IV)
                (5) Albert Liholiho (died age four)
        (3) Grace Kamaʻikuʻi Young m. Thomas C. B. Rooke (no issue)
        (3) John Young, Jr. (Keoni Ana), m. Julia Alapaʻi Kauwa (no issue)
        (3) Jane (Gini or Kini) Lahilahi Young (aunt of Jane Lahilahi Nuʻuanu)
            m. Joshua Kaʻeo
            (4) Peter (Kekuaokalani) Kaʻeo (no issue)
            (4) Keliʻimaikaʻi (Alebada) Kaʻeo (no issue)
        (3) Jane (Gini or Kini) Lahilahi Young
            (4) Albert Kūnuiākea (by Kamehameha III) m. Mary Poli
                (no known issue)

 *Notes*

Prologue

1. "Snow" is a nautical term for a vessel very much like a brig, which has square rigged sails on a foremast and a mainmast, but a snow has a small third mast carrying a trysail. This rig seems to have been preferred at the time for maximum in-shore maneuverability with a small crew (Richards, *Captain Simon Metcalfe*, p. 184).
2. Alexander, *Brief History of the Hawaiian People,* p. 22.

Chronology

1. This is somewhat speculative, despite the conviction of other biographers that Young did indeed sign on the *Eleanora* in 1787. It is a fact that he was with the vessel when it left Macao for the Northwest Coast of North America in 1789.

Chapter 1 • *The World of 1744*

1. See David L. Gregg to Colonel William P. Young in Hawaiian Historical Society 32nd Annual Report, pp. 51–53. The original letter is in the Hawai`i State Archives.
2. Particularly, in recent years, by George W. Collins of Honolulu.

Chapter 2 • *Enter the* Eleanora

1. Stokes, *Nationality of John Young,* p. 19.
2. *Paradise of the Pacific,* July–August 1937.
3. Gregg, letter to Colonel William P. Young.
4. For Metcalfe's letter, see chapter 7.
5. Gregg, letter to Colonel William P. Young.
6. In his journal of 1825, the Reverend Artemis Bishop tells of spending the evening with Young, then eighty, at his Kawaihae home. Bishop wrote: "He is an Englishman by birth, but followed the sea for many years out of Philadelphia, was in the confidence of his employers, and expected to be raised soon to the command of a vessel."
7. Howay, *Journal of Captain James Colnett.*
8. *United States Naval Records of the American Revolution,* p. 243.
9. Henry G. Despard, "Times and Tides of Simon Metcalfe," unpublished manuscript. In my search for information on John Young and his association with Metcalfe, I wrote to Mr. Despard. In his reply (April 21, 1995) he wrote: "I know only that he [John Young] had—previous to joining the crew of the *Eleanora*—been boatswain of the *Prince of Wales*." I then wrote Despard asking if he could kindly provide documentation of any kind for his statement. But before he could reply the angel of death intervened.
10. Richards, *Captain Simon Metcalfe,* pp. 5ff.

Chapter 3 • *Tracking the Trader*

1. Documented in "Rapport de Mer" (Declaration of Sea Reports), Royal Admiralty Court, Port Luis, Isle of France, F 10/215, March 9, 1792. Metcalfe's testimony was that he left New York on February 18, 1787. Mauritius Archives, F 10/215; see Richards, *Captain Simon Metcalfe,* p. 173. The same testimony states: "After touching at Madera [*sic*], Mohilla [*sic*], Trinkmale, Carical, Pondichery [*sic*], Calcutta, Malacca and Batavia [they] arrived in the month of August."

2. Richards, *Captain Simon Metcalfe*, p. 10.

3. Ibid., p. 56.

4. Ibid., p. 41.

5. Boit, *Journal of Voyage around the Globe*, October 18, 1795.

6. Townsend, *Voyage of the Neptune*, diary entry for August 20, 1798.

7. Records of the East India Company, Canton Factory, Consultations, G/12/89, August 1788. India Records Office, London.

8. Despard, "Times and Tides of Simon Metcalfe," p. 89.

Chapter 4 • Who Bought Colnett's Bosun?

1. Richards, *Captain Simon Metcalfe*, p. 97.

2. Despard, "Times and Tides of Simon Metcalfe."

3. Ibid., p. 91.

4. George W. Collins was a prominent businessman in Honolulu who, like Despard, was taken up with the story and mystery surrounding John Young and made exhaustive studies with the intention of publishing a book. Whereas Despard completed his manuscript, Collins died before completion of his work. But he left behind reams of drafts, copies of letters, and countless notes. Much of his correspondence was with researchers in Liverpool and London. He was most thorough in his pursuit of facts, even traveling to England to seek information.

Collins also opines that Young may have been impressed into the service of the British navy, undoubtedly served on a privateer, and also may have seen service in the African slave trade.

5. Howay, *Journal of Captain James Colnett*, p. vi.

6. Ibid., p. xii.

7. Ibid., p. xiii.

8. I commissioned at least four professional researchers in Liverpool and London to search the archives of the Public Records Office, the British Library, the East India Company, and British naval records. Nothing on Young was found, and nothing significant on Colnett.

9. Collins, notes and papers.

10. Barnard, *Narrative,* p. 220.

Chapter 5 • Macao to the Northwest

1. Several locales and time frames are drawn from Richards' partly fictive *Captain Simon Metcalfe—Pioneer Fur Trader.* Also see Henry Despard's "Times and Tides of Simon Metcalfe."

2. Despard, "Times and Tides of Simon Metcalfe," p. 92.

Chapter 6 • Massacre on Maui

1. A picul weighs 133.3 pounds avoirdupois and is the Chinese unit generally used in reference to Hawaiian trade. The pleasant odor of sandalwood, especially when burned, added to its value. In addition to its importance to Chinese Buddhists for religious purposes, it also has medicinal value and is used for cosmetics. Trinkets of various sorts are made from its fragrant wood. Sandalwood was imported to China in the sixth century from India and the East Indies. The Hawaiian supply was depleted in the early 1800s by overzealous chiefs whose greed for money and gifts worked to their disadvantage.

2. Vancouver, *Voyage of Discovery.*

3. Kahananui, *Ka Mooolelo Hawaii*, pp. 176–79.

4. *Columbian Centinel* (Boston), November 30, 1791.

5. Ibid.

6. Alexander, *Brief History of the Hawaiian People*, p. 82.

7. Vancouver, *Voyage of Discovery*, vol. 2, p. 140.

8. Ibid.

Chapter 7 • Seizure at Sea

1. Vancouver, *Voyage of Discovery*, vol. 2, p. 137.

2. Townsend, *Voyage of the Neptune*, p. 59.

3. Alexander, *Brief History of the Hawaiian People*, p. 127: "Kameeiamoku, a high chief of Kona, was insulted and beaten with a rope end by Metcalfe for some trifling offense, on which he had vowed to revenge himself on the next vessel that should come into his power."

Collins manuscript, p. 2: "By coincidence the chief of the village [Ka'ūpūlehu] had planned, ever since the elder Metcalfe had struck him with a knotted rope, to seize the first foreign ship that came along. And there she lay—"The Fair American"! Going aboard with his warriors, and simulating a friendly attitude to cloak his evil design. . . ."

Dibble, *History of the Hawaiian Islands*, vol. 2: *Hawaiian Spectator*, January 1839: "A flogging which Kameeiamoku received on board a ship [*Eleanora*] was the cause of the capture. He said 'If a vessel comes in my way, destruction be to it.' "

London, *Our Hawaii*, pp. 263ff: "Following this [an unsubstantiated fracas aboard the *Eleanora*] a high alii of Kona was insulted and thrashed with a rope by Capt. Metcalfe for some trifling offense, and vowed vengeance on the next ship that should come within his reach."

Richards, *Captain Simon Metcalfe*, p. 125: "The Capture of a Sloop: A flogging which Kameeiamoku received on board a ship was the cause of the capture. He said 'If a vessel comes in my way, destruction be to it.' "

4. Ingraham, *Journal of the Voyage of the Brigantine Hope*. The original journal is in the Library of Congress, Washington, D.C.; a copy is in the Bishop Museum, Honolulu.

5. Vancouver, *Voyage of Discovery*, vol. 2, p. 138.

6. Ibid., pp. 139–40.

7. Ibid., p. 140.

8. Terry Ku 'Awhao Wallace, personal interview, August 10, 1997.

9. Vancouver, *Voyage of Discovery*, vol. 2, p. 137. Metcalfe and his ship had already departed Kealakekua and were China bound before Kamehameha sought to return the schooner. As far as is known, Metcalfe never learned of the fate of Thomas and the *Fair American*.

10. Data on Davis is scant. Little is known, aside from his having been born in Wales and having been the only survivor on the *Fair American*. It is a fact that he was cared for and treated kindly by Kamehameha. Like Young, this man was just what the king had been seeking, a person skilled in the use of modern arms and warfare. Like his English colleague, he participated in the skirmishes and battles that eventually brought victory to Kamehameha. See Day, *History Makers of Hawaii*, pp. 32ff.

Davis married twice, the first wife, Hikone, being a relative of Kamehameha (ibid.). Between his first wife and Ha'ale, his second, three children survived: Elizabeth (Betty or Peke), Sarah (Kale), and George Hū'eu. The Davis name and Davis blood are still quite prominent in the Islands, especially on Hawai'i Island. After Isaac's death, believed to be by poisoning, Young and his wife, Kaoanaeha, took in the three juveniles as part of their own family. It is believed that Davis died in Honolulu and was buried in the vicinity of what is now King and Piikoi Streets (Terry Ku 'Awhao Wallace, personal interview, June 8, 1997).

Chapter 8 • Detained or Kidnapped?

1. Barnard, *Narrative*, pp. 219ff. All quotes from Barnard are from this source.
2. Vancouver, *Voyage of Discovery*, vol. 2, p. 135.
3. Ibid.
4. Fornander, *History of the Hawaiian People*, vol. 1.
5. Vancouver, *Voyage of Discovery*, vol. 2, pp. 136ff.
6. Ibid.
7. Fornander, *History of the Hawaiian People*, vol. 1.
8. Metcalfe's letter is the oldest item among many thousands in the Hawai'i State Archives. It found its way there with many documents from the Foreign Office of the Kingdom of Hawai'i when that office was dissolved. It had been turned over to Robert Wyllie, Foreign Minister, by Dr. Thomas C. B. Rooke, John Young's son-in-law. Presumably Young acquired the letter from the unknown party who received it on the shore of Kealakekua Bay. Judging from its many creased folds, it must have been carried personally by Young, for at the time he had only his musket and the clothes on his back, no sea chest or knapsack. It is in fragile condition.
9. Cartwright, *Some Early Foreign Residents of the Hawaiian Islands*, p. 58.
10. Ibid., pp. 59–60.
11. Ibid., pp. 62–63.
12. Ingraham, *Journal of the Voyage of the Brigantine Hope.*

Chapter 9 • King of Kings

1. "The Polynesians divided the year into two seasons, winter (rainy) and summer (dry). The beginnings of the seasons were regulated by sunset and the appearance of certain stars. The full year was divided into twelve periods of thirty days each, each month given a name. Days, like those in ancient Rome or Greece, were divided into three parts; morning, midday, and afternoon. Nighttime was calculated by five separate 'stations'" (Fornander, *History of the Hawaiian People*, vol. 1, pp. 118ff).
2. Kamakau, *Chiefs of Hawaii*, pp. 66–68.
3. Kuykendall, *Hawaiian Kingdom*, vol. 1, p. 429.
4. Stokes, *Nationality of John Young.*
5. Hawaiian Historical Society Reprint, no. 44, p. 44.
6. Pole, *First King*, p. 11.
7. Ibid., p. 16.
8. Kamakau, *Chiefs of Hawaii*, p. 84.
9. Kuykendall, *Hawaiian Kingdom*, vol. 1, p. 31.
10. Ii, *Hawaiian History*, p. 7.
11. Kuykendall, *Hawaiian Kingdom*, vol. 1, p. 63.
12. Ibid., p. 29.
13. Ibid.
14. Townsend, *Voyage of the Neptune*, p. 4.
15. Ibid., p. 5.
16. Beaglehole, *Captain James Cook*, p. 476.
17. Fornander, *History of the Hawaiian People*, vol. 1, p. 171.
18. Kahananui, *Ka Mooolelo Hawaii.*
19. Kamakau, *Chiefs of Hawaii*, p. 97.
20. Kuykendall, *Hawaiian Kingdom*, vol. 1, p. 31.
21. Day, *History Makers of Hawaii*, p. 66.
22. Kamakau, *Chiefs of Hawaii*, p. 143.

23. Kuykendall, *Hawaiian Kingdom*, vol. 1, p. 20.

24. *The Friend* (Honolulu), July 1894, p. 52.

25. Hawaiian Historical Society 30th Annual Report, 1922, p. 37.

26. Kuykendall, *Hawaiian Kingdom*, vol. 1, p. 32.

27. Pole, *First King*, p. 175.

Chapter 10 · Foiled

1. Captain Colnett makes no mention of either Young or Davis by name in his journal, nor does he allude to an attempt to rescue them. His entry for April 2, 1791 (in Howay, *Journal of Captain James Colnett*), refers only to learning that several Europeans who had deserted their vessels were with Kamehameha and that "I sent two notes to them." It must be noted, however, that Colnett's journal is somewhat "jerky" and disconnected. There are apparent omissions of items worthy of note.

2. Quotations in this chapter are from Vancouver, *Voyage of Discovery*, vol. 2, pp. 141–42.

   Vancouver wrote: "I shall proceed to state in the abstract, the report made to me both by Young and Davis. . . . I have not any doubt as to the veracity of either"(idem, p. 135). A simpler version is that recorded by Edward Bell, clerk aboard the *Chatham*, Vancouver's armed tender. In his writing of their second visit to Hawai'i (1793), Bell relates the account of the *Fair American* and continues: "Sometime after this affair, Young and Davis both, were rescued by ToMaiha Maiha's hands, at a time when they were on the point of being put to death by Tiana, for endeavoring to effect their escape off the island on board the Argonaut, Captn. Colnett" (idem, p. 141).

Chapter 11 · To the Victor . . .

1. Kuykendall, *Hawaiian Kingdom*, vol. 1, p. 35.

2. Kamakau, *Chiefs of Hawaii*, p. 150.

3. Kuykendall, *Hawaiian Kingdom*, vol. 1, p. 36.

4. The following excerpt appeared in the July 1921 issue of the monthly bulletin of the Hawaiian Volcano Observatory. It gives as its source "Mr. Thomas G. Thrum [who] kindly sent . . . the following translation from the Hawaiian, Kamakau's *Mooolelo*": "The sand and stones sprang up and became a pillar, standing up higher than the mountains of Mauna Loa and Mauna Kea. Those who lived at Kawaihae shore (northwest coast of Hawai`i) saw this wonderful fire pillar standing in the sky, and at the top of this pillar a flame of fire was flashing (lapalapa, a flashing as of lightening)."

5. Kuykendall, *Hawaiian Kingdom*, vol. 1, p. 36.

6. Kamakau, *Chiefs of Hawaii*, p. 150.

7. Doyle, *Makua Laina*, p. 68.

8. Kuykendall, *Hawaiian Kingdom*, vol. 1, p. 37.

9. Ibid.

10. Ibid., p. 38.

11. Kamakau, *Chiefs of Hawaii*, p. 156.

12. Kuykendall, *Hawaiian Kingdom*, vol. 1, p. 38.

13. Kamakau, *Chiefs of Hawaii*, p. 158.

14. Besides Young and Davis, these would have included Thomas, Ridler, Mackey, and two other seamen named Evans and James. See Bloxam, *Diary*, p. 94 (May 3, 1825). Related to him by "Old Young" in July 1825.

15. Bishop, *Journals and Letters*, p. 141.

16. In 1907, 112 years after the island of O'ahu fell to Kamehameha, the Daughters of Hawai'i unveiled a tablet on the site of the Nu'uanu battle. The unveiling took place

with appropriate ceremonies attended by a considerable number of the society's members, women of Hawaiian blood. The tablet is made of gray marble and is set in a niche cut into the rocky face of the *pali*, near the turn of the Old Pali Road. Its inscription reads: "Erected by the Daughters of Hawai'i, 1907, to commemorate the Battle of Nu'uanu, fought in this valley, 1795, when the invading conqueror, Kamehameha I, drove the forces of Kalanikupule, King of O'ahu, to the pali and hurled them over the precipice, thus establishing the Kamehameha dynasty." Two hundred years after the battle, in April 1995, hundreds of Hawaiians trekked from Waikiki, by torchlight, for a sunrise ceremony at the *pali*. The purpose of this great out-turning was to "reconsecrate the site where up to ten thousand Hawaiian warriors may have died two centuries ago in a battle to unite the people of Hawaii" (*Honolulu Advertiser*, April 30, 1995).

       It is interesting to note that John Young, who played a crucial role in the historic battle, is buried in the Royal Mausoleum, less than a mile away from the plaque and battle site.

17. Boit, *Voyage around the Globe*, p. 74.

Chapter 12 • *The Vancouver Visits*

1. Day, *History Makers of Hawaii*, p. 123.
2. Kuykendall, *Hawaiian Kingdom*, vol. 1, pp. 39ff.
3. Fornander, *History of the Hawaiian People*, vol. 1, p. 336.
4. Unless noted otherwise, quotations in this chapter are from Vancouver, *Voyage of Discovery*, vol. 2, pp. 122–68.
5. Restarick, *Viewpoint of a Bishop*, p. 12.
6. Vancouver, *Voyage of Discovery*, vol. 3, p. 65.
7. Puget, Journal, January 13, 1794.
8. Restarick, *Viewpoint of a Bishop*, p. 12.
9. Ibid., pp. 12–13.
10. Kuykendall, *Hawaiian Kingdom*, vol. 1, p. 42.
11. Ibid., p. 43.

Chapter 13 • *'Olohana at Home*

1. Meares, "Voyage Made in Years 1788–89."
2. Kane, *Ancient Hawaii*, p. 31.
3. Thrum, *Hawaiian Annuals*, p. 101.
4. Apple, *Pahukanilua*, p. 47.
5. Judd, "Sketches of Life," p. 36.
6. Kotzebue, *Voyage of Discovery*, pp. 329–30.
7. Ibid., p. 295.
8. Chamisso, *Voyage around the World*.
9. Iselin, *Trading Trip*.
10. Kotzebue, *Voyage of Discovery*, p. 334.
11. Freycinet, *Hawaii in 1819*.
12. Ellis, *Journal*, pp. 55ff.
13. Ibid., p. 71.
14. Ibid., p. 73.
15. Ibid., p. 286.
16. Puget, Journal.

Chapter 14 • The Russians Are Coming!

1. Lisiansky, *Voyage around the World*, pp. 102ff.
2. Emerson, *Honolulu Fort*, pp. 12ff.
3. Kuykendall, *Hawaiian Kingdom*, vol. 1, p. 56.
4. Chamisso, *Voyage around the World*, vol. 3, p. 291.
5. Day, *History Makers of Hawaii*, pp. 7ff.
6. Daws, *Shoal of Time*, p. 52.
7. Kotzebue, *Voyage of Discovery*, p. 322.
8. Kuykendall, *Hawaiian Kingdom*, vol. 1, p. 58.
9. Hawaiian Historical Society, Paper 6, p. 12.
10. Kuykendall, *Hawaiian Kingdom*, vol. 1, p. 58.
11. Emerson, *Honolulu Fort*, p. 19.
12. Kuykendall, *Hawaiian Kingdom*, vol. 1, p. 59.

Chapter 15 • Royal Rite of Passage

1. Kamakau, *Chiefs of Hawaii*, p. 210.
2. Kane, *Voyagers*, p. 120.
3. Charlot, *Choris and Kamehameha*, pp. 10ff.
4. Campbell, *Voyage around the World*, pp. 126–27.
5. Choris, *Voyage pittoresque*, p. 3.
6. Kotzebue, *Voyage of Discovery*, pp. 193–94.
7. Charlot, *Choris and Kamehameha*, p. 23.
8. Kamakau, *Chiefs of Hawaii*, pp. 210ff.
9. Golovnin, *Tour around the World*.
10. Kuykendall, *Hawaiian Kingdom*, vol. 1, p. 60.
11. Kamakau, *Chiefs of Hawaii*, p. 211.
12. Daws, *Shoal of Time*, pp. 53–54.
13. Kamakau, *Chiefs of Hawaii*, p. 180.
14. Daws, *Shoal of Time*, p. 54.
15. Townsend, *Voyage of the Neptune*, pp. 26–27.
16. Barrere, *King's Mahele*, p. 25.
17. Kamakau, *Chiefs of Hawaii*, pp. 211ff.
18. Bingham, *Residency of Twenty-one Years*, p. 71. Bingham writes that he drew his account from a translation by natives that was published in *Ka Mooolelo Hawaii* in 1838.
19. Pole, *First King*, p. 186.
20. Ibid.
21. Ibid., p. 187.
22. Barrere, *King's Mahele*, p. 26.
23. Kamakau, *Chiefs of Hawaii*, p. 215.

Chapter 16 • The Coming of the Calvinists

1. James Hunnewell (in *The Friend*) says their arrival was on March 30, 163 days out of Boston. Gavan Daws (*Shoal of Time*, p. 64) also says March 30, 159 days. A. Grove Day (*History Makers of Hawaii*) gives March 31. Way off was the English missionary William Ellis (*Journal*, p. 21), who wrote that it was February 4.
2. *Missionary Album*, p. 7.
3. Ibid., p. 62.
4. Ibid., p. 17.

5. Daws, *Shoal of Time*, p. 103.

6. Day, *History Makers of Hawaii*, p. 133.

7. Bailey, *Kings and Queens*, p. 73.

8. Bingham, *Residency of Twenty-one Years*.

9. Ibid.

10. *The Friend* (Honolulu), January 1864, p. 5.

11. Kamakau, *Chiefs of Hawaii*, pp. 246–47.

12. "The Arrival of the Missionaries."

13. "The *Thaddeus* Journal," p. 32.

Chapter 17 • Character References

1. Vancouver, *Voyage of Discovery*, vol. 2, p. 160.

2. Ibid., pp. 166ff.

3. Kuykendall, *Hawaiian Kingdom*, vol. 1, p. 43.

4. Vancouver, *Voyage of Discovery*, vol. 2, p. 169.

5. Puget, Journal, 1793.

6. Kuykendall, *Hawaiian Kingdom*, vol. 1, p. 43.

7. Manby, *Journal*.

8. Macrae, *With Lord Byron*, pp. 36–38.

9. Ingraham, *Journal of the Voyage of the Brigantine Hope*.

10. Iselin, *Trading Trip*, p. 64.

11. Turnbull, *Voyages in the Pacific*, pp. 225–26.

12. Ibid.

13. Withington, *Golden Cloak*, pp. 65ff.

14. Ibid.

15. Greenwell, *House of Young*, p. 9.

16. Menzies, *Hawaii Nei*, p. 96.

17. Thurston, *Life and Times*, p. 202.

18. Withington, *Golden Cloak*, p. 77.

19. Stokes, *Nationality of John Young*, pp. 16ff.

20. Doyle, *Makua Laina*, p. 132.

21. Clarice Taylor, *Honolulu Star Bulletin*, September 15, 1960.

22. Ibid.

23. Bishop, *Tour of Hawaii*, p. 49.

24. Taylor, *Honolulu Star Bulletin*, May 18, 1960.

25. It is questionable that Kamehameha became a teetotaler at that time, 1791, or even later. Turnbull tells of Young and Davis considering leaving their chief because "he was so peculiarly mischievous when inflamed with liquor" and "our lives become endangered as often as you are [intoxicated] then no longer master of yourself." Apparently Kamehameha accepted this "reproof and made an engagement on the spot, that for the future he would never exceed a certain fixed and moderate quantity; and this engagement he most inviolably adhered." Turnbull concluded: "Such instances of self-control are rarely seen, even among the most polished nations of Europe." (Turnbull, *Voyages in the Pacific*, p. 228.)

26. Thrum, *Hawaiian Annual*, 1878, p. 33.

27. Withington, *Golden Cloak*, p. 72.

Chapter 18 • Evensong

1. Bailey, *Kings and Queens*, p. 81.

2. Taylor, *Honolulu Star Bulletin*, September 7, 1960.

3. Macrae, *With Lord Byron*, p. 36.

4. Bishop, *Reminiscences of Old Hawaii*, p. 24.

5. Alexander, *Brief History of the Hawaiian People*.

6. Reynolds, Journal.

7. Ibid.

8. Chamberlain, Journal, vol. 20, p. 7.

9. Ibid.

10. Pohukaina was on the premises of the present Iolani Palace grounds. Some remains are still entombed there, but their identity is uncertain. A grass-covered mound, surrounded by a black iron fence, marks this first Royal Mausoleum. A bit of Hawai'i's ancient respect and reverence for the departed is preserved by an embossed metal plaque on the gate, which reads KAPU.

11. *Hawaiian Gazette*, November 6, 1865.

12. *Pacific Commercial Advertiser*, November 4, 1865.

Chapter 19 • The Family

1. A couple of people made phone calls indicating a relationship, but failed to return calls with more information. Rather interesting is the matter of William Pa'akaula Kalawai'anui of Waimea, who, in a land dispute with Parker Ranch, wrote a letter to the *Hawaii Tribune-Herald* (June 18, 1996) in which he claimed to be a "direct descendant of John Young." The elderly Mr. Kalawai'anui declined the author's request to discuss the lineage in any way. Jane Lahilahi, the daughter of Kānehoa and Ha'ale, married a man named Nu'uanu. They had a son named Samuel. If he had offspring, which is not known, the blood line of John Young may have survived. (Genealogy Book no. 28, Bishop Museum, Honolulu.)

2. The letter is in the Hawai'i State Archives. Mr. Holms would be Oliver Holmes, at one time the assistant governor of O'ahu. He left a family of six children who inherited portions of land given him by Kamehameha.

3. Taylor, *Honolulu Star Bulletin*, February 1, 1960.

4. Kamakau, *Chiefs of Hawaii*, p. 257.

5. Day, *History Makers of Hawaii*, p. 70.

6. Macrae, *With Lord Byron*, pp. 6–7.

7. Collins, notes and papers.

8. *Polynesian*, October 11, 1851.

9. *Hanai* means to nourish, feed, support, or adopt. It is the latter meaning of the word that is used here. It is still not uncommon for Hawaiian parents to allow a newborn child to be raised by other adult relatives or close friends. It is not a system that requires adoption papers.

10. Day, *History Makers of Hawaii*, p. 133.

11. Taylor, *Honolulu Star Bulletin*, April 5, 1960.

12. Ibid.

13. Peter Young Ka'eo was an intelligent child and attended the Chiefs' Children's School. Unfortunately, he developed Hansen's disease and was sent to the leprosy settlement at Kalaupapa, from which he was later discharged. Through the years he and his cousin, Queen Emma, among others, communicated frequently, and many of the letters have been preserved and published in *News from Molokai* by Alfons Korn.

14. She was also a chiefess, known by the name of Kaoanaeha.

15. Davis had been dead for fifteen years. His three children, informally adopted by John Young and Kaoanaeha, were by now all adults.

16. The Mahele came about after Kamehameha III was persuaded by Westerners to

abandon traditional land ownership by adopting the European and American concept of private property. More or less, by the stroke of a royal pen, the lands of the Hawaiian archipelago were divided among the king, chiefs, crown, and commoners, with the latter getting the least. It was "an event which was second only to the arrival of the Europeans in its impact on Hawai'i. In a matter of a few years Hawai'i changed from a society in which the king served as steward of the land that belonged to the gods, to one which he, the alii, or the nobility, and the maka aina or commoners, acquired outright ownership of the land" (Fitzpatrick and Moffat, *Surveying the Mahele,* fly leaf).

17. Barrere, *The King's Mahele.*
18. Stokes, *Nationality of John Young,* p. 15.

Chapter 20 · Queen Emma

1. Peterson, *Notable Women,* p. 120.
2. Waldron, *Liholiho and Emma,* pp. 4ff.
3. Day, *History Makers of Hawaii,* p. 2.
4. Benton, *Beloved Queen,* p. 48.
5. Peterson, *Notable Women,* p. 120.
6. Benton, *Beloved Queen,* p. 17.
7. Waldron, *Liholiho and Emma,* p. 21.

Chapter 21 · Will the Real John Young Please Stand Up?

1. Foremost was John F. G. Stokes, who, in the 1930s, responded to some of the inquiries received by Bishop Museum. Unless otherwise noted, the bulk of information in this chapter is extracted from his *Nationality of John Young, a Chief of Hawaii,* which appeared in the Hawaiian Historical Society's 1938 Annual Report.
2. It is tantalizing that the location of the flood was not identified by Stokes, assuming that he knew it. Presumably Young had his papers with him in his last months when living with his son-in-law, Dr. Rooke. Years later Rooke obligingly turned over a great number of historical documents to the Archives of Hawai'i. Among them may have been the existing forty-two pages from Young's journal. They are mostly brief daily observations; nothing is said about his nationality. Stephen Reynolds reports a great flooding in Nu'uanu Valley on April 10, 1844. Rooke owned property in Nu'uanu, in addition to his Union Street and Beretania properties, and may have been living there, with the Young papers, at the time of the flood.
3. Vancouver, *Voyage of Discovery,* vol. 2, p. 283.
4. Restarick, *Viewpoint of a Bishop.*

Epilogue · The Old Homestead

1. The majority of information in this chapter is extracted from "Excavations of John Young's Residence in Kawaihae" by Paul H. Rosendahl and Laura Carter Schuster.
2. Hawaiian Historical Society Annual Report, 1929, p. 60.

Appendix I · Louis Choris's Account of John Young's Life

1. Young was seventy-three at the time. He lived for another eighteen years.
2. The *Eleanora* actually waited at least until March 22, the date of Captain Metcalfe's letter to the men on shore.

Bibliography

Abbreviations

BM   Bishop Museum
HMCS   Hawaiian Mission Children's Society
HHS   Hawaiian Historical Society
UHP   University of Hawai'i Press

Alexander, W. D. *A Brief History of the Hawaiian People.* New York: American Book Company, 1891.

———. *Proceedings of the Russians on Kauai.* Paper no. 6. Honolulu: HHS, 1894.

Apple, Russell A. *Pahukanilua: Homestead of John Young.* Honolulu: National Park Service, 1978.

"The Arrival of the Missionaries." Translated by Dorothy Barrere. Lahainaluna Paper, no. 4, Doc. 606. Lahaina: Lahainaluna Press, 1842.

Bailey, Paul. *Those Kings and Queens of Old Hawaii.* Tucson, Ariz.: Westernlore Press, 1975.

Barnard, Captain Charles. *A Narrative of the Sufferings and Adventures of Captain Charles H, Barnard during the Years 1812–1816.* New York: J. Lindon, 1829.

Barrere, Dorothy B. "Kamehameha in Kona." *Pacific Anthropology,* no. 23. Honolulu: BM, 1975.

———. *The King's Mahele: The Awardees and Their Land.* Volcano, Hawai'i: privately published, 1994.

Beaglehole, J. C., ed. *The Journals of Captain James Cook: The Voyage of the Resolution and Dicovery 1776–1780.* Cambridge: Cambridge University Press, 1967.

Benton, Russell E. *Emma Naea Rooke, Beloved Queen of Hawaii.* Queenstown, Ont.: Edwin Mellen Press, 1988.

Bingham, the Reverend Hiram. *A Residency of Twenty-one Years in the Sandwich Islands.* 1858. Reprint, Rutland, Vt.: Charles F. Tuttle, 1981.

Bishop, Artemas. "Tour of Hawaii." *Missionary Herald,* February 1827.

Bishop, Charles. *Journals and Letters, 1794–99.* Edited by Michael Roe. Cambridge: Cambridge University Press, 1966.

Bishop, Sereno. *Reminiscences of Old Hawaii.* Honolulu: Hawaiian Gazette, 1916.

Bloxham, Andrew. *Diary, 1824–25.* Special Publication 10. Honolulu: BM, 1925.

Boit, John, Jr. *The Journal of a Voyage around the Globe, 1795–1796.* Edinburgh. HMCS photocopy.

Campbell, Archibald. *A Voyage around the World from 1806 to 1812.* 1822. Reprint, Honolulu: UHP, 1967.

Carter, G. R. "More of John Young." In *Some Early Foreign Residents of the Hawaiian Islands.* Honolulu: HHS 25th Annual Report, 1916.

Cartwright, Bruce, Jr. *Honolulu in 1809–1810: Paradise of the Pacific.* Honolulu: no publisher, n.d.

———. *Some Early Foreign Residents of the Hawaiian Islands.* Honolulu: HHS 25th Annual Report, 1916.

Chamberlain, Levi. Journal, 1822–49. Volume 20. HMCS, 1937.

Chamisso, Adelbert von. *A Voyage around the World with the Romanzov Exploring Expedition, 1815–1818.* Translated and edited by Henry Kratz. Honolulu: UHP, 1986.

Charlot, Jean. *Choris and Kamehameha.* Honolulu: BM Press, 1958.

Choris, Louis. *Voyage pittoresque autour du monde.* Paris: Iles Sandwich, 1822.

Cleveland, R. J. *A Narrative of Voyages and Commercial Enterprises.* 1842. Reprint, New York: Harper Bros., 1886.

Collins, George. Notes and papers for his unpublished "Life of John Young," now in possesion of his son, George Collins, Jr., of Kailua-Kona, Hawai'i.

Daws, Gavan. *Shoal of Time.* New York: Macmillan, 1968.

Day, A. Grove. *History Makers of Hawaii.* Honolulu: Advertiser Publishing Company, 1953.

Despard, Henry G. "The Times and Tides of Simon Metcalfe." Manuscript, 1995.

Dibble, Sheldon. *History of the Sandwich Islands.* Lahaina: Lahainaluna Press, 1843.

Doyle, Emma Lyons. *Makua Laina.* Honolulu: Advertiser Publishing Company, 1953.

Ellis, William. *Journal of William Ellis, Missionary from the Society and Sandwich Islands.* 1917. Reprint, Honolulu: Advertiser Publishing Company, 1963.

Emerson, Dr. N. B. *History of the Honolulu Fort.* Honolulu: HHS Annual Report, no. 8, 1900.

Fitzpatrick, Gary, and Riley Moffat. *Surveying the Mahele.* Honolulu: Editions Limited, 1995.

Fornander, Abraham. *Ancient History of the Hawaiian People to the Time of Kamehameha I.* 1885. Reprint, Honolulu: Mutual Publishing Company, 1996.

Freycinet, Louis Claude Desaules de. *Hawaii in 1819: A Narrative Account.* Translated by E. L. Wiswell. Edited by Marian Kelly. Honolulu: Pacific Anthropological Records, no. 26, BM, 1978.

The Friend. Monthly publication of the Hawaiian Evangelical Association, Honolulu.

Golovnin, Vasili Mikhailovich. *Tour around the World on the Sloop-of-War Kamschatka, 1817–19.* St. Petersburg, 1822. Translated by Joseph Barth in *The Friend* (Honolulu), July and August 1894.

Greenwell, Alice. *The House of Young.* Smithtown, N.Y.: Exposition Press.

Gregg, David L. Letter to Colonel William P. Young, August 30, 1856. Honolulu: HHS 32nd Annual Report, 1923.

Henriques, Edgar. *John Young the Englishman*. Honolulu: HHS 25th Annual
   Report, 1916.
Howay, Judge F. W. *The Journal of Captain James Colnett aboard the Argonaut*.
   Toronto: Champlain Society, 1940.
Hunnewell, James. Letter in *The Friend* (Honolulu), January 1864.
Ii, John Papa. *Fragments of Hawaiian History*. Honolulu: BM Press, 1959.
Ingraham, Joseph. *Journal of the Voyage of the Brigantine Hope, 1790–92*.
   Reprint no. 3. Honolulu: HHS, 1918.
Iselin, Isaac. *Journal of a Trading Trip around the World, 1805–08*. New York:
   McIlroy and Emmet, n.d.
Janion, Aubrey. *The Olowalu Massacre*. Honolulu: Island Heritage, 1976.
Judd, Bernice. *Voyages to Hawaii before 1860*. Honolulu: UHP, 1974.
Judd, Laura Fish. "Sketches of Life in the Hawaiian Islands, 1828–61."
   Honolulu Star Bulletin, March 18, 1928.
Kahananui, Dorothy M., editor and translator. *Ka Mooolelo Hawaii*. Lahaina:
   Lahainaluna Press, 1838. Reprint, Honolulu, 1984.
Kamakau, S. M. *Ruling Chiefs of Hawaii*. English translation, 1961. Revised
   edition, Honolulu: Kamehameha Schools Press, 1992.
Kane, Herb Kawainui. *Ancient Hawaii*. Captain Cook, Hawai'i: Kawainui Press, 1997.
———. *Voyagers*. Honolulu: Whalesong, 1991.
Korn, Alfons. *News from Molokai: Letters between Peter Kaeo and Queen Emma*.
   Honolulu: UHP, 1976.
Kotzebue, Captain Otto von. *A Voyage of Discovery 1815–18 in the Ship Rurick*.
   London: Longman, Hurst, Rees, Orme and Brown, 1821.
Kuykendall, Ralph S. *The Hawaiian Kingdom*. Volume 1. 1938. Reprint,
   Honolulu: UHP, 1968.
Lisiansky, Urie. *A Voyage around the World*. 1812. English translation, London:
   J. Barth, 1814.
London, Charmain. *Our Hawaii*. New York: Macmillan, 1922.
Lyman, Henry M. *Hawaiian Yesterdays*. Chicago: A. C. McClurg and Company,
   1906.
Macrae, James. *With Lord Byron at the Sandwich Islands in 1825*. Edited by
   William F. Wilson. Hilo: Petroglyph Press, 1972.
Makemason, Maud W. *The Land of Kokoiki and the Birthday of Kamehameha the
   First*. Report no. 49. Honolulu: HHS, 1936.
Manby, Thomas. *Journal of 1793*. Ed. W. F. Wilson. Honolulu: Honolulu
   Mercury, 1929.
McGuire, M. B. *The Vancouver Story*. New York: Vantage Press, 1977.
Meares, John. "Voyage Made in Years 1788–89 from China to the North West
   Coast of America." Sale, London: J. Walters, 1791.
Menzies, Archibald. *Hawaii Nei 128 Years Ago*. Honolulu, 1920.
Miller, A. P. Letter regarding Young family records, December 21, 1934.
Missionary Album. HMCS Sesquicentennial Edition. Honolulu: Edwards
   Enterprises, 1969.

New York Daily Advertiser, February 18, 1787. New-York Historical Society.

Peterson, Barbara Bennett. *Notable Women of Hawaii.* Honolulu: UHP, 1984.

Pole, James T. *Hawaii's First King.* New York: Bobbs-Merrill, 1959.

Puget, Peter. Journals, 1793–94. Photocopies in HMCS.

Restarick, Henry B. *Hawaii in 1778 to 1920 from the Viewpoint of a Bishop.* Honolulu: Paradise of the Pacific, 1924.

———. *Historic Kealakekua Bay.* Paper no. 15. Honolulu: HHS, 1928.

Reynolds, Stephen. Journal, 1829–1855. Manuscript. HMCS.

Richards, Rhys. *Captain Simon Metcalfe—Pioneer Fur Trader.* Fairbanks, Alaska: Limestone Press, 1991.

Rosendahl, Paul H., and Laura Carter Schuster. "Excavations of John Young's Residence in Kawaihae." Tucson, Ariz.: National Park Service, Western Archaeological and Conservation Center, 1988.

Schuster, Laura Carter. "Bulldozers and Achaeology at John Young's Homestead." Manuscript. Honolulu: National Park Service, 1992.

Stokes, John F. G. *Nationality of John Young, a Chief of Hawaii.* Honolulu: HHS 47th Annual Report, 1938.

Taylor, Alfred Pierce. *Under Hawaiian Skies.* Honolulu: Honolulu Advertiser Publishing Company, 1926.

Thrum, Thomas. *Hawaiian Annuals.* Honolulu: Queen Emma Museum/ Daughters of Hawai`i.

Thurston, Lucy. *Life and Times of Mrs. Lucy G. Thurston.* 1882. Reprint, *The Friend* (Honolulu), 1934.

Townsend, Ebenezer. *The Voyage of the Neptune around the World in 1796–1799.* Reprint no. 4. Honolulu: HHS, 1921.

Turnbull, Captain John. *Voyages in the Pacific Ocean 1802–04.* 2nd ed. London: W. McDowall, 1814.

United States Naval Records of the American Revolution. Washington, D.C.: Naval Archives, n.d.

Vancouver, Captain George. *Voyage of Discovery to the North Pacific Ocean and round the World.* Volumes 2 and 3. 1798. Reprint, New York: Plenum Publishing Company, 1967.

Wahlroos, Sven. *Mutiny and Romance in the South Seas.* Topsfield, Mass.: Salem House Publishers, 1989.

Waldron, Elizabeth. *Liholiho and Emma.* Revised ed., Honolulu: Daughters of Hawai'i, 1986.

Westervelt, W. D. *Kamehameha's Method of Government.* Honolulu: HHS Annual Report, no. 30, 1921.

Withington, Antoinette. *The Golden Cloak.* Honolulu: Hawaiiana Press, 1953.

Young, John. Journal of John Young with entries for years 1808, 1809, 1821, 1825. Manuscript. Honolulu: Hawai'i State Archives.

 *Index*

Young, James Kānehoa (son), 13, 104, 133, 143–46, 148, 168, 177n.

Young, Jane (Gini or Kini) Lahilahi (daughter), 13, 107, 143–46, 148, 168

Young, Jane Lahilahi (granddaughter), 143, 168, 177n.

Young, John ('Olohana), 11–13, 16–20, 22, 24–27, 29–32, 37, 40–42, 46–57, 62, 64–65, 67–73, 76, 82, 83, 86–96, 98–117, 119, 120, 122, 123, 127–50, 153, 155–68, 171n.–174n., 176n.–178n.
   family of, 13, 102, 104–8, 138, 142–48, 155–56, 168
   journal of, 18, 105, 109, 127, 135, 163, 178n.
   lands of, 102, 104–6, 146–48, 158, 162–64

Young, John (of Conn.), 160

Young, John (of Mass.), 158

Young, John, Jr. (Keoni Ana) (son), 13, 107, 144–45, 147–48, 155, 168

Young, Julia Alapaʻi Kauwa (daughter-in-law), 144, 168

Young, Kānehoa. *See* Young, James Kānehoa

Young, Kaoanaeha (Mary) (2nd wife), 13, 105, 107, 134, 135, 144, 146–49, 158, 163, 167, 168, 171n., 177n.

Young, Keliʻimaikaʻi (Alebada) Kaʻeo. *See* Kaʻeo, Keliʻimaikʻi (Alebada)

Young, Namokuelua (1st wife), 13, 104, 107, 168

Young, Otis, 158

Young, Peter (brother), 17, 135, 168

Young, Rebecca (of Mass.), 158

Young, Robert (father), 16, 17, 160, 168

Young, Robert (son), 13, 104, 142, 168

Young, Sarah (Kale) Davis (daughter-in-law), 143, 146–48, 168, 171n.

Young, Col. W. P., 19

Young, Zerviah Huntington (of Conn.), 160

About the Author

Emmett Cahill grew up in western New York State. He came to Hawai'i in the 1940s, where he was first stationed on Maui during World War II. After the war he returned to Hawai'i and spent twenty-two years at the Hawaiian Telephone Company. He took early retirement in 1968, then served as executive director of several nonprofit organizations in Honolulu. In 1985 he moved to Volcano, on the Big Island of Hawai'i, and took up a career as a writer. He is the author of *Hawaiian Stamps: An Illustrated History, Yesterday at Kalaupapa,* and *The Shipmans of East Hawai'i,* and he is currently researching a history of Hawai'i's Royal Mausoleums.